Annabel **Karmel's**
NEW COMPLETE
Baby and Toddler
Meal Planner

Annabel **Karmel's**
NEW COMPLETE
Baby and Toddler
Meal Planner

Over 200 quick, easy and healthy recipes

ANNABEL KARMEL

Illustrations by Nadine Wickenden

EBURY PRESS
LONDON

10 9 3 7 6 5 4 3 2 1

First published by Ebury Press in 1991
Reprinted eighteen times between 1991 and 2001

This Tenth Anniversary Edition published in 2001 by
Ebury Press
an imprint of The Random House Group Ltd
Random House
20 Vauxhall Bridge Road, London SW1V 2SA
www.randomhouse.co.uk

The Random House Group Limited Reg. No. 954009

A CIP catalogue record for this book is available from
the British Library

ISBN: 0 09 188088 2

AN EDDISON•SADD EDITION
Edited, designed and produced by
Eddison Sadd Editions Limited
St Chad's House
148 King's Cross Road
London WC1X 9DH

This edition edited by SP Creative Design
Wickham Skeith, Suffolk

Phototypeset in Baskerville MT using
QuarkXPress on Apple Macintosh
Origination by Columbia Offset, Hong Kong
Printed in Great Britain by Bath Press Colourbooks, Glasgow

*This book is dedicated
to my children,
Nicholas, Lara and Scarlett,
and to the memory of
my first daughter,
Natasha.*

CONTENTS

INTRODUCTION

Like any other besotted young mother, I wanted the very best for my babies. As a food lover and cordon bleu cook, I wanted them to enjoy the wonderful tastes and aromas of fresh foods. With common sense, extensive research, cooperative infants and a tolerant husband I knew I could create delicious recipes. Prepared quickly and easily they would be better for babies and toddlers than commercial vitamin- and iron-fortified powders and bland processed purées with a shelf-life of over two years.

Poor nutrition can cause problems that will plague our children for the rest of their lives. A recent government study found that as many as two-thirds of cancer cases are linked to the type of food that people eat. The untimely death of my first child Natasha at the age of thirteen weeks was the catalyst that spurred me into writing this book, which has now become such a valuable and popular, practical guide to parents all over the world.

Battles over the dinner table are one of the more dubious pleasures of parenthood. Blessed is the mother who has never encountered the tenacious iron will of a child who will not eat. I now have three children and the pleasure of seeing them enjoy my foods has been a wonderful experience. I am reassured to know that they are eating good fresh produce not over-processed convenience foods.

At a time when diet is most crucial to our child's health, why should most meals emanate from jars and packets? There is no great mystique to making your own baby food, and nothing can be better than home-cooked purées made from good-quality fresh, natural ingredients. Don't be overwhelmed by the impressive lists of nutritional information on the labels of commercial baby foods: your own will contain the same goodness but without any added starches (like maltodextrin, which is the same substance that provides the glue on envelopes and stamps!).

Not only do home-made purées taste like real food, they also work out much cheaper. Even busy working mums can give their baby the best start in life, since foods like mashed banana, avocado and papaya make excellent no-cook baby purées. You can plan your baby's menus ahead and, in just a couple of hours, prepare a whole month's food supply for your baby, freezing extra portions in ice-cube trays. You can also turn many baby purées into delicious soups for the rest of the household by adding stock and seasoning, and many family meals such as a chicken casserole with vegetables can be suitable for your baby if you set aside a portion and cook it without salt or spices.

In early childhood, eating habits and tastes (good or bad) are formed for life, so by introducing your baby to a wide range of fresh, stimulating flavours you will help establish a healthy eating pattern. Commercial carrot purées always taste the same, but with home-made purées babies get used to the natural variations in the taste of home-cooked food, which helps them to adapt to family meals as they grow up.

I give feeding guidelines, but there are no hard and fast rules since every baby develops at his or her own pace. Children need calories to grow as well as an adequate supply of proteins, vitamins and minerals. This is best provided by a good varied diet. Although a low-fat, high-fibre diet is fine for adults, it is not appropriate for young children. Babies should not have salt added to their food, but salt in moderation after one year is unlikely to do any harm.

If there are rules – and rules are made to be broken – they are to aim for:

- Fresh food
- Low sugar
- Low animal fat
- Low salt (no salt before one year).

A baby in the home is an opportunity to look at the dietary rules for the whole family. Some of these recipes are so delicious I serve them when entertaining! Babies' nutrition in their first year probably has a greater influence than at any other time of life. This reinforces the need to start early with a good balanced diet. When your child opts for the raw fruits and vegetables (which adults imagine kids hate) over sugary sweets, you will recognise your success.

Good luck. I hope you and your child enjoy many happy meals together!

CHAPTER ONE

THE BEST FIRST FOODS FOR YOUR BABY

Many mothers feel that, once their baby is three months old, they should be starting to feed him solids. In fact there is no 'right' age as every baby is different. Physiologically, there is no rush to get your baby started on solids. A baby's digestive system is not fully matured for the first few months and foreign proteins very early on may increase the likelihood of allergic food problems later. However, be warned: socially there is a kind of competitive spirit amongst mothers to get their child on to puréed steak and chips as soon as possible! I would advise that, provided your child is satisfied and growing properly, you should wait until he is between four and six months old before starting to give him simple solid foods.

MILK IS STILL THE MAJOR FOOD

It is very important to remember when starting your baby on solids that milk is still the most natural and the best food for growing babies. I would encourage mothers to try breastfeeding. Apart from the emotional benefits, breast milk contains antibodies that will help protect infants from infection. In the first few months, they are particularly vulnerable and the colostrum a mother produces in the first few days of breastfeeding is a very important source of antibodies which help to build up a baby's immune system. (If only for this reason, it is obvious that there are enormous benefits in breastfeeding your child even for as little as one week.) It is also medically proven that breastfed babies are less likely to develop certain diseases in later life.

Milk should contain all the nutrients your baby needs to grow. There are 65 calories in 120 ml/4 fl oz milk, and formula milk is fortified with vitamins and iron. Cow's milk is not such a 'complete' food for human babies so is best not started until your baby is one year old. Solids are introduced to add *bulk* to a baby's diet, and to introduce new tastes, textures and aromas; they also help the baby to practise using the muscles in his mouth. But giving a baby too much solid food too early may lead to constipation, and provide fewer nutrients than he needs. It would be very difficult for a baby to get the equivalent amount of nutrients from the small amount of solids he will consume as he gets from his milk.

Do not use softened water or repeatedly boiled water when making up your baby's bottle, because of the danger of concentrating mineral salts. Babies' bottles should not be warmed in a microwave, as the milk may be too hot even though the bottle feels cool to the touch. Warm bottles by standing them in hot water.

There is no fixed rule as to how much milk a baby should consume during the day. However, it is important to make sure (especially as it is highly likely that a bottle may not be finished at each feed) that, up to the age of five months, your baby drinks milk at least four times a day. If the number of feeds is reduced too quickly, your baby will not be able to drink as much as is needed. Some mothers make the mistake of giving their baby solid food when he is hungry, when what he really needs is an additional milk feed.

Although most babies of six months are perfectly able to drink pasteurised cow's milk, and many mothers, especially in other countries, start their babies on cow's milk this early, it is best to continue with breast or formula milk for one year.

Dairy products like yoghurt, *Petit Suisse* and cheese can be introduced any time after six months and are generally very popular with babies. Choose whole-milk products as opposed to low-fat.

FRESH IS BEST
Fresh foods just do taste, smell and look better than jars of pre-prepared baby foods. Nor is there any doubt that, prepared correctly, they are better for your baby (and you), for it is inevitable that nutrients, especially vitamins, are lost in the processing of pre-prepared baby foods. Home-made foods taste different from the jars you can buy. I believe your child will be less fussy and find the transition to joining in with family meals easier if he is used to a wide selection of fresh tastes and textures from an early age.

ORGANIC
Organic fruit and vegetables are produced without artificial chemicals, such as pesticides and fertilisers. However, organic produce is unlikely to taste better, and there is no scientific evidence that pesticide levels in ordinary fruits and vegetables are harmful to young babies and children. It is an environmentally friendly option but generates higher prices and it is up to you to decide whether it's worth the extra money.

GM FOODS
Genetic modification(GM) is the process of transferring genes from one species to another. For example, a tendency to resist frost could be implanted from one plant to

another. Currently 25% of the world's food crops are lost through insect attack every year; that's enough food to feed one billion people. Genetic modification could create a crop that is resistant to damage from particular insects. More research is needed to know whether genetic modification can improve the quality and availability of crops or whether the cost to humans and the environment outweigh any benefit.

YOUR BABY'S NUTRITIONAL REQUIREMENTS

The following essential nutrients are needed for a healthy diet and promoting growth.

Proteins

Proteins are needed for the growth and repair of our bodies; any extra can be used to provide energy (or is deposited as fat). Proteins are made up of different amino acids. Some foods (meat, fish, soya beans and dairy produce, including cheeses) contain all the amino acids that are essential to our bodies. Other foods (grains, pulses, nuts and seeds) are valuable sources of protein but don't contain all the essential amino acids.

Carbohydrates

Carbohydrates and fat provide our bodies with their main source of energy. There are two types of carbohydrate: sugar and starch (which in complex form provides fibre). In both types there are two forms: natural and refined. The natural form provides a more healthy alternative.

SUGARS	
Natural	Fruits and fruit juices Vegetables and vegetable juices
Refined	Sugars and honey Soft drinks Sweet jellies Jams and other preserves Biscuits and cakes
STARCHES	
Natural	Wholegrain breakfast cereals, flour, bread and pasta Brown rice Potatoes Dried beans and lentils Peas, bananas and many other fruits and vegetables
Refined	Processed breakfast cereals (e.g. sugar-coated flakes) White flour, breads and pasta White rice Sugary biscuits and cakes

Fats

Fats provide a concentrated source of energy. The body also needs to store some fat in order to prevent excessive loss of body heat. Thus a certain amount of fat is essential in everyone's diet. Foods that contain fats also contain the fat-soluble Vitamins A, D, E and K. The problem is that many people eat too much fat and the wrong type of fat.

There are two types of fat – saturated, which mainly comes from animal sources, and unsaturated, which comes from vegetable sources. It is the saturated fats which are the most harmful and which may lead to high cholesterol levels and coronary disease later in life.

It is important to give your baby whole milk for at least the first three years but try to reduce fats in cooking and use butter and margarine in moderation. Try to reduce saturated fats in your child's diet by cutting down on red meat, especially fatty meats like lamb; replace them with more chicken and fish. This may in fact be a good time to review the whole family's eating habits, and to cut out all that butter on Daddy's toast in the morning!

FATS	
Unsaturated	Sunflower, grapeseed, safflower, sesame, soya, rapeseed and olive oils Soft polyunsaturated margarine Oily fish (e.g. mackerel)
Saturated	Butter Meat Lard, suet and dripping Eggs Cheese and full-fat yoghurt Cakes and biscuits Hard margarine Whole milk

Vitamins and Minerals

The possibility of vitamin deficiencies in the developed world should not be ignored. The children most at risk are those who follow a vegan diet (no animal products at all) and those drinking cow's milk from the age of six months. Paediatricians recommend that these children should take a daily vitamin supplement until they are at least two years old.

For most children, eating fresh food in sufficient quantity and drinking formula milk until the age of a year, vitamin supplements are probably unnecessary.

There are two types of vitamins – water-soluble (C and B complex) and fat-soluble (A, D, E and K). Water-soluble vitamins cannot be stored by the body, so foods containing these should be eaten daily. They can also easily be destroyed by overcooking, especially when fruits and vegetables are boiled in water. You should try to preserve these vitamins by eating the foods raw or just lightly cooked (in a steamer, for instance).

There is some controversy over whether vitamin supplements can improve your child's IQ. As vitamins are necessary for the correct development of the brain and nervous system, it is important that a good supply of all vitamins is taken. A good balanced diet should supply all that is required and an excess of vitamins is potentially harmful. However, children who are picky eaters could benefit by taking a supplement specially designed for children that contains a full range of vitamins.

VITAMIN A

Essential for growth, healthy skin, tooth enamel and good vision.

Liver
Oily fish
Carrots
Dark green vegetables (e.g. broccoli)
Sweet potatoes
Oranges
Squash
Tomatoes
Lentils
Watercress
Apricots and peaches
Whole milk and eggs
Butter and margarine

VITAMIN B COMPLEX

Essential for growth, for changing food into energy, for a healthy nervous system and as an aid to digestion. There are a large number of vitamins in the B group. Some are found in many foods, but no foods except for liver and yeast extract contain them all.

Meat, especially meat juices (so use in gravy) and liver
Fish
Dairy produce and eggs
Wholegrain cereals
Wheatgerm
Dark green vegetables
Potatoes
Yeast extract (e.g. Marmite)
Nuts
Dried beans
Bananas

VITAMIN C

Needed for growth, healthy tissue and healing of wounds. It helps in the absorption of iron.

Vegetables such as: broccoli, Brussels sprouts, greens, sweet peppers, potatoes, spinach, cauliflower
Fruits such as: oranges and other citrus fruits, blackcurrants, melon, papaya, strawberries, tomatoes

VITAMIN D

Essential for proper bone formation, it works in conjunction with calcium. It is found in few foods, but is made by the skin in the presence of sunlight.

Oily fish
Liver
Oils
Eggs
Margarine
Dairy produce

VITAMIN E

Important for the composition of the cell structure, and helps the body to create and maintain red blood cells.

Vegetable oils
Margarine
Wheatgerm
Nuts

VITAMIN K

Aids in blood clotting, maintains bones and is present in the intestine. It is found in most vegetables and wholegrain cereals.

CALCIUM

Calcium is needed for strong bones, good teeth and growth.

Dairy produce, especially milk
Canned fish with bones (e.g. sardines, but only for older children)
Dried fruit
Bread and flour
Broccoli
Pulses

IRON

Iron is needed for healthy blood and muscles. A deficiency in iron is probably the most common and will leave your child feeling tired and run-down.

Liver and red meat
Oily fish
Egg yolks
Dried fruits (especially apricots)
Wholegrain cereals
Lentils and dried beans
Green leafy vegetables
Chocolate

Water

Humans can survive for quite a time without food, but only a few days without water. Babies lose more water through their kidneys and skin than adults and also through vomiting and diarrhoea.

Thus it is very important that your baby should not be allowed to dehydrate. Make sure he drinks plenty of fluids. Cool, boiled water is the best drink to give your baby, on hot days particularly, as it will cool the body down quicker than any sugary drink.

It is really not necessary to give a very young baby anything to drink other than milk or plain water if he is just thirsty. Fruit syrups, squashes and sweetened herbal drinks should be discouraged, to prevent dental decay. Don't be fooled if the packet says 'dextrose' – this is just a type of sugar.

If your baby refuses to drink water, then give him unsweetened baby juice or fresh 100 per cent fruit juices. Dilute according to instructions or, for fresh juice, use one part juice to three parts water, gradually increasing to half and half.

THE QUESTION OF ALLERGIES

It is fairly common for babies to inherit food allergies from their parents and, where there is a history of a particular food allergy, that food should only be introduced singly and with great care.

The commonest foods which carry a risk of allergic reaction in babies are cow's milk and dairy products, eggs, fish (especially shellfish), some fruits, nuts, and foods containing gluten. Some babies (and older children) can also react to artificial food colourings and additives. The commonest allergic problems which may be triggered by adverse reactions to food are: nausea; vomiting; diarrhoea; asthma; eczema; hayfever; rashes and swelling of the eyes, lips and face. This is one reason why it is unwise to rush starting your baby on solid foods.

There is no need to be unduly worried about food allergies, unless there is a family history. The incidence of food allergy in normal babies is extremely small and, with the tendency to a later introduction of solid food between four and six months, they have become even less common. However, it is still children under the age of eighteen months who are most likely to develop an allergy to a particular food. Although a lot of children 'grow out of it' by the age of two, some food allergies – particularly a sensitivity to eggs, milk, shellfish or nuts – can last for life. If your child has an allergy, do tell friends' parents and the school when he is old enough.

Never be afraid to take your baby to the doctor if you are worried that there is something wrong. Young babies' immune systems are not fully matured and babies can become ill very quickly if they are not treated properly and can develop serious complications.

Lactose Intolerance

Lactose intolerance is not actually an allergy. Children who suffer lactose intolerance lack the substance lactase, an enzyme present in the superficial layers of the small bowel, which breaks lactose down to simpler sugars. Lactose is present in all milks and these babies will not be able to drink breast or cow's milk. A soya formula is given.

Sometimes children who are lactose-intolerant are able to eat dairy products like cheese and yoghurt with no ill effects.

Cow's Milk Protein Allergy

If your baby is sensitive to cow's milk, consult your doctor who will probably recommend a soya-based milk formula. Unmodified soya milk is not suitable as it is nutritionally inadequate. However, some babies who are allergic to cow's milk are also allergic to soya-based milks, and for those babies there are a number of hypoallergic milk formulas available on prescription. Breast milk is the best alternative for babies who are allergic to cow's milk, but mothers may need to limit dairy foods themselves as these can be transferred to their baby through breast milk.

No dairy products are tolerated in this condition, and in the weaning diet milk-free vegetable or soya margarine may be substituted for butter, and carob for milk chocolate. Very often babies outgrow this allergy by the age of two.

Eggs

Eggs can be given from six months but they must be thoroughly cooked until both the white and the yolk are solid. Soft-boiled eggs can be given after one year.

Fruits

Some children can have an adverse reaction to citrus and berry fruits. Rosehip or blackcurrant, being rich in Vitamin C, make good alternatives to orange.

Honey

Honey should not be given to children under twelve months as it can cause infant botulism. Although this is very rare, it is best to be safe as a baby's digestive system is too immature to deal with the bug.

Nuts

It is rare to be allergic to tree nuts such as walnuts and hazelnuts. However, peanuts can cause a severe allergic reaction. In families with a history of any kind of food allergy, avoid all products containing peanut until the child is about three years old. Where there is no history of allergic disorders, peanut butter can be used after the age of one year.

Because of the danger of inhalation, whole nuts should not be given to young children under five years of age. Even ground nuts should be avoided for at least the first seven months.

Gluten

If there is a family history of gluten intolerance, babies under six months *must* follow a gluten-free diet, but it is preferable for all young babies. Gluten is found in wheat, rye, barley and oats, and gluten sensitivity can cause coeliac disease which, although rare, can be serious.

When buying baby cereals and rusks, choose varieties that are gluten-free. Baby rice is the safest to try at first, and thereafter there are plenty of alternative gluten-free products such as soya, corn, rice, millet and potato flours for thickening and baking, brown rice, rice noodles, buckwheat spaghetti, etc.

PREPARING BABY FOODS

Preparing and cooking baby foods is not difficult, but, because you are dealing with a young baby, considerations like hygiene must be of the utmost importance.

Equipment

Most of the equipment required will already be in your kitchen – mashers, graters, sieves, etc. – but the following three pieces I consider are vital!

Mouli This hand-turned food mill with variable cutting discs purées the food, separating it from the seeds and tough fibres which can be difficult for the baby to digest. It is ideal for foods like dried apricots, sweetcorn or green beans.

Blender or food processor This is useful for puréeing larger quantities. However, foods for young babies will often need to be

sieved afterwards, before serving, in order to remove any indigestible seeds and skin.

Steamer The best way to preserve the taste and vitamins in fruits and vegetables is to cook them in a steamer. It is worth buying a multi-tiered steamer, enabling you to cook several different foods at once. (A colander over a saucepan, with a well-fitting lid, is a cheaper alternative.)

Sterilising

At first, it is very important to sterilise bottles properly, and particularly the teats that your baby sucks, by whatever approved method you choose. Warm milk is the perfect breeding ground for bacteria and, if bottles are not properly washed and sterilised, your baby can become very ill. It is also best to sterilise the dishes and spoons you use for feeding your baby. It would be impossible, however, to sterilise *all* the equipment you use for cooking and puréeing baby food, but take extra care to keep everything very clean.

Use a dishwasher if you have one; the water is at a much higher temperature than it would be possible to use if washing the utensils by hand and helps to sterilise your equipment. However, once it is removed from the dishwasher, it does not remain sterile; bottles should be filled with milk immediately and stored in the fridge. Dry utensils with kitchen paper rather than a non-sterile tea towel.

All milk bottles should continue to be sterilised until your baby is one year old, but there is really not much point sterilising spoons or food containers beyond the age when your baby crawls and puts everything in reach into his mouth.

Cooking Baby Foods

Fruits and vegetables can lose nutrients when they are cooked, so it makes sense to eat some cooked and some raw. However, raw ones would be difficult to digest for a young baby, so, until the age of six months, most fruit and vegetables (apart from ripe bananas, papaya, peaches, nectarines and avocados) should be cooked. As the baby gains teeth and learns to chew, the fruit or vegetables can be cooked more lightly in order to retain Vitamin C and crispness. After about six months, your baby can have purées of raw fruit and fresh grated fruit; raw or very *al dente* vegetables can be given as a finger food.

Cook in many ways – boiling, steaming, microwaving, stewing or baking. Try to avoid fat-based methods of cooking such as frying (or cut down on the amount of fat used). Steaming and microwaving are by far the best methods to maximise on nutritional benefits. The water in which, or over which, vegetables have cooked (so long as it does not contain salt) could be used as a drink or as the cooking water for something else, such as pasta. Try also to maximise on fuel economy; steam a number of different foods at one time before puréeing and storing separately.

Cook fruit and vegetable purées for your baby by whichever method you choose. In each case make sure the purée is completely smooth, with no lumps. Later on you can adjust the texture of the purée to suit your baby as he starts to chew. Freeze any purée you are not using straight away.

Boiling or steaming Wash fruits or vegetables carefully; peel, seed or stone as necessary and cut into small pieces. Add just enough water to cover and simmer until tender, or steam (about 10 minutes; see individual recipes). Drain or remove from steamer, retaining the cooking water, then blend, mouli or mash, adding some of the cooking water or a little formula or breast milk to bring it to the correct consistency for your baby.

Microwaving Wash and peel, seed or stone the fruits or vegetables as necessary and cut into slices. Put in a suitable microwave dish with a little water or milk (2 tablespoons for 100 g/4 oz vegetables). Cover, leaving an air vent, and microwave on High for about 3 minutes. Uncover,

stir, re-cover and cook for another 2 minutes or until tender. Cooking times will vary according to how hard the fruits or vegetables are to begin with. Blend, mash or mouli to the right consistency, adding water as necessary.

Freezing Baby Foods

Whenever possible, prepare more food than is immediately needed and freeze the remainder in ice-cube trays for future meals. There are a limited number of foods that do not freeze well (like bananas and avocados) but most can be frozen with excellent results. Thus, in 1 or 2 hours, you can prepare enough to feed your baby for a month – making for a happier mother and baby and more time to spend together. Throughout this book, the snowflake symbol denotes recipes that are suitable for freezing.

You will need a freezer which can freeze food to –18°C (0°F) or below in 24 hours, and sterile packaging. At the earliest stages, when only teaspoons of food are being taken, this means plastic ice-cube trays (sterilise these as well) and polythene freezer bags.

FREEZER STORAGE TIME	
Fruits	*6 months*
Vegetables	*6 months*
Purées with milk	*4–6 weeks*
Fish	*10 weeks*
Red meat and chicken	*10 weeks*

Cook and purée the food as described in the recipes, cover, leave to cool, then freeze until hard in ice-cube trays. Knock out and store in clearly labelled freezer bags. Label the food with the expiry date, so you never give your baby food that is past its best.

To thaw one meal, remove the relevant number of cubes of food from the bag (only one at the very beginning) and leave at room temperature for an hour. Heat thoroughly, cool, then serve immediately. If using a microwave, stir well to make sure there is an even distribution of heat, and allow to cool. Always test the temperature of food before giving it to your baby. Fruits to be served cold can defrost in the refrigerator overnight.

Never refreeze meals which have already been frozen, and never reheat them more than once.

INTRODUCING NEW FOODS

I have listed below when you should introduce particular foods to your baby. This is not an exhaustive list and you should refer to each chapter for more information.

WHEN CAN THEY HAVE ...?	
Apple, pear, banana, papaya	*4–5 months*
Carrot, cauliflower, potato, courgette, squash, green beans, swede, sweet potato	*4–5 months*
Dried fruit, peach, kiwi, apricot, plum, melon, avocado	*5–6 months*
Peas, tomato, spinach, celery, leek, parsnip, sweet pepper	*5–6 months*
Foods containing gluten	*6 months*
Eggs	*6 months*
Fish	*6 months*
Chicken, dairy products	*6 months*
Citrus fruit, berries, mango	*6–7 months*
Mushroom, sweetcorn	*6–7 months*
Other meats	*6–12 months*
Split pea, butter beans, lentils	*8–9 months*
Shellfish	*over 2 years*

MEAL PLANNERS

In the next chapter I have devised some meal planners which will help you through the first weeks when you start to wean your baby. However, there are endless variations on the foods that can be given and the order in which they can be introduced.

It is also worth noting that some babies may prefer to have solids at lunch-time rather than breakfast. And, if your baby's last meal is close to bedtime, avoid giving him anything heavy or difficult to digest. This is certainly not the time to experiment with new foods if you both want a good night's sleep.

I have tried to give a wide choice of recipes, although I expect that, in practice, meals that your baby enjoys would be repeated several times – and this is where your freezer will come in handy.

In each subsequent chapter, there are meal planners for your baby which you may follow or simply use as a guide. Adapt the charts according to what is in season and what you are preparing for your family. From nine months onwards, you should be able to cook for your baby and family together, perhaps eating the recipes you give your baby for lunch and tea for your own supper, provided you do not add salt to your baby's portion before one year.

In these later charts, I have set out four meals a day, but many babies are satisfied with three meals and some healthy snacks.

Many of the vegetable purées in the early chapters can be transformed into a vegetable soup; and a number of the vegetable dishes can serve as good side dishes for the family. Again, if you give the baby some of the vegetables you are preparing for the family, make sure they have not been salted. In the later chapters many recipes are suitable for the whole family.

After each recipe is a symbol of two faces – one smiling, the other gloomy – each with a tick box. You will find these useful in recording your successes (or otherwise)!

CHAPTER TWO

FOUR TO SIX MONTHS AND WEANING

In the recent past there was a lot of pressure on parents to start their babies on solid food much earlier than four months – this pressure was variously commercial, medical and social (keeping up with the Jones's baby!). Ideas have now changed and this is all to the good, for many quite ordinary foods, as already discussed, can cause allergies. Neither is a baby's digestive system capable, until at least four months old, of absorbing foods more complex than baby milk.

WHEN TO START WEANING

Every baby is different and some larger babies may just not be getting enough to satisfy them. Your baby will let you know when she needs to start solids; if, for example, she is no longer satisfied after a 250 ml/8 fl oz bottle; if the interval between feeds becomes shorter over a prolonged period, or if she starts becoming unsettled during the night. Another sure sign is when she reaches out and tries to chew everything in sight!

THE FIRST SOLID FOODS

'Solids' is a strange word for the mush we give our babies and is a little misleading.

Try only *one food at a time* at the very beginning. Offer apple purée, for instance, for a couple of days before giving her pear or banana. In that way, if there is a reaction, you will know what caused it. Later on, you can make it all more interesting by *combining* different foods.

The other vital point is *not to reduce the milk intake*. Milk is still the most important factor in her growth and development.

On pages 38–41 I have set out some feeding charts, which will help you when you start to wean your baby. Use these charts as a guide, adapting them according to what is in season and what you are preparing for your family.

Rice

Initially I would advise one of the commercial baby rice cereals. These, although refined, are enriched with vitamins and iron (check the label) and they should also be free of sugar and salt. (This information will be printed on the packet. In fact this is a good time to start reading the lists of contents of all packets, jars and cans to look out for undesirables.) Baby rice is also easily digested. Make it up with baby milk or cooled boiled water according to the instructions on the packet.

Fruit

Since most babies are born with a sweet tooth (breast milk is naturally sweet), you should have no trouble in getting your baby to enjoy eating fruit. Fruit that is fully ripe is naturally sweet. If you think a purée is sour-tasting, you can add a little apple juice. Remember, though, that the baby may actually prefer something less sweet than you and that is all to the good!

Most fruits provide Vitamin C and minerals, and the yellow fruits contain Vitamin A. At first a baby should have cooked purées of fruits like apples and pears, or uncooked mashed banana or papaya. At about six months, your baby can graduate to other raw mashed fruits: pears, melon, peaches, grapes and plums are all delicious as long as they are ripe.

Fresh fruits are best, but fruits canned in their own juice or water (*not* in a syrup) could also be used. Dried fruits should be introduced later and in small quantities; although they are nutritious they tend to be a laxative. If you are worried about the

use of pesticides, organic fruit and vegetables are available. However, it is always best to wash, and peel where appropriate, all fruit and vegetables before giving them to babies.

Vegetables

Some people prefer to start their babies on vegetables rather than fruit. Because most babies will take to eating fruit quite happily, they feel it is important to establish a liking for more savoury tastes.

At the beginning, when introducing a baby to solids, it is best to start with root vegetables, particularly carrots, since they are naturally sweet. Different vegetables provide different vitamins and minerals (for instance, green vegetables provide Vitamin C, and yellow provide Vitamin A) so a variety is of value at later stages.

Many vegetables have quite strong flavours – broccoli, for example – so when solids are fairly well established, you could mix in some potato or baby rice and milk to make it more palatable. Very young babies like their food quite bland.

Note that all fruit and vegetables can also be cooked in a microwave (see page 17 for general method).

TEXTURES

At the very beginning of weaning, the rice and fruit or vegetable purées should be fairly wet and soft. This means that most vegetables, for instance, should be cooked until very soft so that they purée easily. You will probably need to thin out the consistency of the purées, since babies are more likely to accept food in a semi-liquid form. You can use formula or breast milk, fruit juice or boiled water.

As your baby becomes more accustomed to the feel of 'solid food' in her mouth, you can gradually start to reduce the amount of liquid that you are adding to the purées, which will encourage her to chew a little. This should be a natural process as she should want to chew her food as she starts teething (usually between six and twelve months). You could also *thicken* the purées if necessary with baby rice or some crumbled rusk. As the baby becomes older and solid feeding is established (at the age of about six months), some fruit can be served raw and vegetables can be cooked more lightly (retaining more Vitamin C). Food can also be mashed or finely chopped to encourage chewing later on.

Remember to peel, core and seed fruits as necessary before cooking and/or puréeing (or put them through a mouli). Vegetables with fibres or seeds should be sieved or put through a mouli for a smooth texture. The husks of leguminous vegetables cannot be digested at this stage.

QUANTITIES

At the very beginning, don't expect your baby to take more than 1–2 teaspoons of her baby rice or a fruit or vegetable purée. For this you should need one portion – in this section, this means a cube from an ice-cube tray. This is approximately 1 tablespoon in volume, but you'll need this much because of spitting and spills!

By the time your baby is six months, she could have graduated to eating 1–2 tablespoons of solids at each meal, which means defrosting *two* frozen food-cubes of the same food.

DRINKS

Water, as outlined on page 13, is the best drink to offer. But freshly squeezed citrus fruits, particularly orange, have a good nutritional value, being high in Vitamin C. Dilute with an equal amount of cooled boiled water. (Never boil citrus juices or they lose their vitamin content.) Apple juice is not so high in Vitamin C as orange juice but is still a good drink. (If your baby reacts to citrus fruit juice, offer blackcurrant or rosehip.)

If buying commercial fruit juices, they should be unsweetened. The bottled fruit juices for babies need to be well diluted according to the instructions on the label. Even pure fruit juices contain intrinsic sugars which can cause tooth decay.

A juicer is a useful machine to have in the kitchen when there is a baby in the house. Many fruits *and* vegetables can be turned into nutritious drinks.

TIPS FOR INTRODUCING SOLIDS

1 Make the rice or purée fairly wet and soft at first, using breast or formula milk, an unsweetened juice or cooking water. A handy tip is to mix the purée in the plastic removable top of a feeding bottle (which has been sterilised).

2 Hold your baby comfortably on your lap or sit her in her baby chair. It would be better if *both* of you were protected against spills!

3 Choose a time when your baby is not frantically hungry and maybe give her some milk first to partially satisfy her – she will then be more receptive to the new idea.

4 Babies are unable to lick food off a spoon with their tongues, so choose a small, *shallow* plastic teaspoon off which she can take some food with her lips. (Special weaning spoons can be bought.)

5 Start by giving just one solid feed during the day, about 1–2 teaspoons to begin with. I prefer to give this feed at lunch-time.

FRUIT AND VEGETABLES

FOUR TO FIVE MONTHS

Apple

Choose a sweet variety of eating apple. Peel, halve, core and slice 2 medium apples. Put into a heavy saucepan with enough water to cover and cook over a low heat until soft (about 7–8 minutes). Or steam over water for the same length of time. Purée.

Apple and Cinnamon

Simmer 2 apples in apple juice or water with a cinnamon stick. Cook as above; remove stick before puréeing.

MAKES 5 PORTIONS

Banana

Mashed banana makes ideal baby food. It is easy to digest and rarely causes allergic reactions. Choose a ripe banana and mash very well with a fork to make it as smooth as possible. Add a little boiled water or baby milk if it is too thick and sticky for your baby to swallow.

If the banana is not ripe enough, split the skin and heat it in the oven or microwave for a couple of minutes to ripen before preparing. Do not freeze bananas.

MAKES 1 PORTION

Pear

Peel, halve and core 2 pears, then cut into small pieces. Cover with a little water, cook over a low heat until soft (about 5 minutes). Or steam over water for the same length of time. Purée.

When your baby is six months or older, there is no longer any need to cook the pear before making it into a purée, provided that the fruit is ripe.

MAKES 5 PORTIONS

Papaya

Papaya is an excellent fruit to give a very young baby. It has a pleasing sweet taste which is not too strong and blends within seconds to a perfect texture.

Cut a medium fruit in half, remove all the black seeds and scoop out the flesh. Purée, adding a little formula or breast milk if you like.

MAKES 4 PORTIONS

24

Cream of Fruit

Combining a fruit purée with baby milk and baby rice or crumbled rusk can make it more palatable for your baby. In the next few months, when your baby may start eating some other exotic fruits like mango and kiwi, this method of 'diluting' the fruit purée with milk will also make them less acidic.

Peel, core, steam or boil and purée the fruit as described and, for each 4-portion quantity of prepared fruit, stir in 1 tablespoon unflavoured baby rice or half a low-sugar rusk and 2 tablespoons baby milk.

MAKES 3 EXTRA PORTIONS

Three-Fruit Purée

This is a delicious combination of three of the first fruits that your baby can eat.

Mix 1 dessertspoon each of pear and apple purées (see page 24) with half a banana, mashed. Later (after six months), you can use half a raw ripe pear, peeled, cored and cut into chunks. Purée this and the half banana in a blender until smooth, then mix together with the dessertspoon of cooked apple purée.

MAKES 4 PORTIONS

Carrot

Peel, trim and slice 2 medium carrots. Place in a pan of lightly boiling water, cover and simmer for about 25 minutes or until very tender. Drain, reserving the cooking liquid and purée to a smooth consistency, adding as much of the reserved liquid as necessary.

The cooking time is longer for small babies. Once your baby can chew, cut the cooking time down to preserve Vitamin C and keep the vegetables crisper.

MAKES 4 PORTIONS

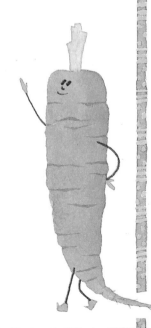

Swede, Parsnip or Turnip

Use half a swede or 100 g/4 oz of parsnip or turnip. Scrub, peel and cut into small cubes. Cover with 175 ml/6 fl oz boiling water and simmer, covered, until tender (about 20 minutes). Drain, reserving the cooking liquid. Mash well with a fork, adding some liquid as necessary.

MAKES 4
PORTIONS

Butternut Squash

Butternut squash has a naturally sweet flavour that is popular with babies.

Peel a butternut squash, weighing about 350 g/12 oz. Remove seeds and cut the flesh into 2.5 cm/1 inch cubes. Steam or cover with boiling water and simmer for about 15 minutes or until tender. Transfer to a blender and make a purée with a little of the cooking liquid.

MAKES 6 PORTIONS

Green Beans

French beans are best since they tend to be less stringy than other varieties. Runner beans should be puréed in a mouli. Wash the beans, top and tail, and remove any stringy bits. Steam until tender (about 12 minutes), then put in a blender and process. Add a little boiled water or baby milk to make a smooth purée. Later on, whole beans make great finger food with a sauce (See Green Fingers, page 92).

Broccoli and Cauliflower

Use 100 g/4 oz of either. Wash well, cut into small florets and add 150 ml/5 fl oz boiling water, Simmer, covered, until tender (about 10–15 minutes). Drain, reserving the cooking liquid. Purée until smooth, adding a little of the reserved liquid (or baby milk) to make the purée into the desired consistency.

Alternatively, steam the florets for 15 minutes for better flavour and retention of nutrients. Once your baby has teeth and can chew, cut the time down to 8–10 minutes to keep the vegetables crisp. Add boiled water or baby milk to make a smooth purée.

MAKES 4 PORTIONS

Courgette

Wash 2 medium courgettes carefully, remove the ends and slice. (The skin is soft, so does not need to be removed.) Steam until tender (about 10–15 minutes), then purée in a blender or mash with a fork. (No need to add extra liquid.)

MAKES 8 PORTIONS

Potato

Carefully wash a 100 g/4 oz potato, removing any blemishes from the skin, then cover with 120 ml/4 fl oz boiling water and simmer until tender (about 20–30 minutes). Peel off the skin, then mouli or mash until smooth. Add enough baby milk to make the purée the desired consistency.

Alternatively, bake a potato in the oven preheated to 200°C (400°F) Gas 6 for about 1 hour or until soft. Scoop out the inside and mouli or mash with a little baby milk. (Later on, keep the baked potato skins, as they are good for babies to chew on when teething.)

Small quantities are most economically cooked in the microwave. Avoid using a food processor to purée potato, as it breaks down the starch to leave a sticky pulp.

MAKES 5 PORTIONS

Cream of Carrot

A creamy purée can be made with many different vegetables by adding milk and baby rice. Make a purée with 75 g/3 oz of carrot (page 25). Mix 2–3 teaspoons unflavoured baby rice with 175 ml/6 fl oz warm baby milk. Vary the amount of rice according to how thick you want the purée. Stir the baby rice mixture into the vegetable purée. Half a low-sugar rusk mixed with milk will also make a creamy purée. Allow the rusk to soften in the baby milk before mixing it into the vegetable purée of your choice.

MAKES 12 PORTIONS

Potato, Courgette and Broccoli

Combining potato with green vegetables makes them more palatable for your baby. Peel and chop a medium potato. Boil in water below a steamer for 15 minutes or until soft. Reduce the heat and steam 1 trimmed and sliced courgette with 25 g/1 oz broccoli florets above the potato for the last 10 minutes of cooking time. Drain the potato and purée with the other vegetables, adding enough baby milk to make a smooth consistency.

MAKES 7 PORTIONS

Broccoli Trio

Potato is used here again to make green vegetables more palatable for your baby. Peel and chop a medium potato and boil in the water below a steamer for 15 minutes until soft. Steam 50 g/2 oz of broccoli and the same of cauliflower florets above the potato for the last 10 minutes. When all the vegetables are tender, purée them in a blender with a dessertspoon of baby milk.

MAKES 14 PORTIONS

Carrot and Cauliflower

Combining vegetables makes them more interesting and, once your baby has got used to carrot and cauliflower separately, this combination makes a nice change. Cook 50 g/2 oz carrots, scraped and sliced, in boiling water for 20 minutes until soft. After 10 minutes, add 175 g/6 oz cauliflower florets. Drain the vegetables and purée in a mouli. Stir in 2 tablespoons baby milk.

MAKES 8 PORTIONS

FRUIT AND VEGETABLES

FIVE TO SIX MONTHS

Peach

Bring a small saucepan of water to the boil. Cut a shallow cross on the skin of 2 peaches, submerge them in the water for 1 minute, then plunge into cold water. Skin and chop the peaches, discarding the stones. Either purée the peaches uncooked or steam first for a few minutes until tender.

MAKES 4 PORTIONS

Cantaloupe Melon

Cantaloupes are the small, very pale green melons with orange flesh. They are rich in Vitamins A and C. Cut in half, remove seeds and scoop out the flesh. Steam for 3–5 minutes, then purée.

Other varieties of sweet melon, so long as they are ripe, can be used too. When your baby is over six months, properly ripe melon may be eaten raw.

MAKES 12–16 PORTIONS

Plum

Skin 2 large ripe plums as for peaches (see opposite). Cut into pieces and bring to the boil in just enough water to cover. Simmer for about 5 minutes or until soft; add sugar to taste if the fruit is a little sour. (Alternatively, steam for about 6 minutes.) Purée, adding as much of the cooking liquid as is necessary to make the purée the desired consistency.

Plums may be eaten raw once your baby is over six months.

MAKES 4 PORTIONS

Apricots and Pears

Fresh apricots have a very limited season but when they are available you should make this delicious combination of fruits. Apricots are rich in Vitamins A and C. Halve and stone 5 fresh ripe apricots. Peel, core and slice 2 ripe pears. Steam the fruit until tender (about 6–8 minutes). When cool enough, skin the apricots. Purée the fruit together in a mouli or blender.

MAKES 12 PORTIONS

Dried Apricot, Peach or Prune

Many supermarkets stock a selection of ready-to-eat dried fruits. Dried apricots are particularly nutritious, being rich in beta-carotene and iron. Cover 100 g/4 oz fruit with fresh cold water, bring to the boil and simmer until soft (about 10 minutes). Drain, remove the stones and press through a mouli to remove the rough skins. Add a little of the cooking liquid to make a smooth purée.

This is good combined with baby rice and milk.

MAKES 4 PORTIONS

Apple and Raisin Compote

Heat 3 tablespoons of fresh orange juice in a saucepan. Add 2 eating apples, peeled, cored and sliced, and 15 g/½ oz of washed raisins. Cook gently for about 10 minutes until soft, adding a little water if necessary. Purée in a mouli to remove seeds and skins.

Dried fruit, even raisins, must always be put through a mouli for a baby.

MAKES 8 PORTIONS

Fresh Peas

Cover 100 g/4 oz podded peas with water, bring to the boil and simmer, covered, until tender (about 10 minutes). Drain, reserving some of the cooking liquid. Put the peas through a mouli or a sieve and add a little of the cooking liquid to make the purée the desired consistency. Best combined with mashed potato and baby milk.

MAKES 4 PORTIONS

Tomatoes

Plunge 2 medium tomatoes in boiling water for 30 seconds. Transfer to cold water, skin and remove the seeds. Cook the flesh in a heavy-bottomed saucepan, mashing over a low heat for about 2 minutes. Put through a mouli or sieve to purée. Combine with baby rice or potato.

MAKES 2–3 PORTIONS

Spinach

Wash 100 g/4 oz spinach leaves very carefully, removing the coarse stalks. Cover with boiling water and simmer, covered, until tender (about 10 minutes). Firmly press out all the excess cooking water and put the spinach leaves through a mouli to purée. Combine with potato.

MAKES 2 PORTIONS

Celery

Wash 100 g/4 oz celery carefully, top and tail, and remove as many strings as possible. Cut into small pieces, cover with boiling water and simmer until tender (about 15 minutes). Drain and put the celery through a mouli. Combine with potato and carrot.

Shredded cabbage can be prepared similarly; but cook for about 10 minutes only.

MAKES 4 PORTIONS

Sweet Red Pepper

Wash a medium pepper. Roast under a grill, quartered, or whole over an open flame (gas hob) until the skin is charred all over. Place in a plastic bag and allow to cool. Core and seed (if not already done), peel off the blistered skin and mouli. Good with cauliflower or potato.

MAKES 2–3 PORTIONS

Avocado

Choose a well-ripened avocado, cut it in half and scoop out the stone. Use 1/3–1/2 and mash the flesh with a fork, maybe adding a little milk. Serve quickly; otherwise it will turn brown.

Do not freeze avocados.

MAKES 1 PORTION

Kiwi and Banana

Kiwi fruits contain almost twice as much Vitamin C as oranges. Make sure you choose a very ripe fruit; otherwise it can be sour.

MAKES 1 PORTION

¼ ripe kiwi, peeled   *¼ ripe banana, peeled*

Purée the kiwi and strain through a fine sieve to get rid of the black seeds. Mash or purée the banana and mix it with the kiwi. Eat straight away or the banana turns brown.

Apple and Banana with Orange Juice

This makes a nice change from plain mashed banana or apple purée. When your baby is six months or older, you can make this with raw grated apple and mashed banana.

MAKES 1 PORTION

¼ apple, peeled, cored and chopped   *1 teaspoon orange juice*
¼ banana, peeled and chopped

Steam the apple until tender (about 10 minutes), then purée or smash it together with the banana and orange juice. Serve as soon as possible.

Peaches, Apples and Pears

This is a good purée to make when peaches are in season. When they are not, it tastes good just with apples and pears.

MAKES 14 PORTIONS

2 eating apples, peeled, cored and chopped
1 cm/½ inch vanilla pod (optional)

2 ripe peaches, skinned and chopped
2 ripe pears, peeled, cored and chopped

Put the apple pieces in a saucepan with 2 tablespoons water and the vanilla pod (if using). Simmer, covered, for about 8 minutes. Add the peaches and pears and cook for 3–4 minutes more. Remove the pod and purée.

Mixed Dried-Fruit Compote

Dried fruits and fresh fruits are delicious combined. You can buy packets of mixed ready-to-eat dried fruit in most supermarkets.

MAKES 12 PORTIONS

50 g/2 oz each dried apricots, dried peaches and prunes

1 eating apple and 1 pear, peeled, cored and chopped, or 1 apple and 3 fresh apricots, skinned, stoned and chopped

Put the dried fruit, apple and pear (or apricot, if using) into a saucepan and just cover with boiling water. Simmer for about 8 minutes. Drain the fruit and purée, adding a little of the cooking liquid if necessary.

Vegetable Stock

Vegetable stock forms the basis of many vegetable recipes. It is well worth making your own supply, which will be free from additives and salt. As a short cut, many supermarkets now stock unsalted vegetable stock in cartons.

MAKES ABOUT 900 ML/1½ PINTS

1 onion, peeled
1 carrot, scrubbed
1 celery stalk
175 g/6 oz mixed root vegetables
(swede, turnip, parsnip, etc.), peeled

25 g/1 oz butter
1 bouquet garni (bought or home-made)
1 sprig of fresh parsley
1 bay leaf
6 black peppercorns

Chop all the vegetables. Melt the butter in a large saucepan and sauté the onion for 5 minutes. Add the remaining ingredients and cover with 900 ml/1½ pints water. Bring to the boil and simmer for about 1 hour. Strain off and discard the vegetables and use the flavoured water as stock.

Carrot and Pea Purée

Both carrots and peas have a naturally sweet taste that appeals to babies.

MAKES 2 PORTIONS

200 g/7 oz carrots, peeled and sliced

40 g/1½ oz frozen peas

Put the sliced carrots in a saucepan and cover with boiling water. Cook, covered, for 15 minutes. Add the peas and cook for a further 5 minutes. Purée with sufficient cooking liquid to make a smooth purée.

Baby Cereal and Vegetables

Sometimes vegetable purées can be very watery – particularly those made from, say, courgettes, which have a high water content. In this recipe I have added baby rice, which makes an excellent thickening agent.

MAKES 10 PORTIONS

25g/1 oz onion, peeled and chopped
1 teaspoon olive oil
1 medium courgette, trimmed and sliced
50 g/2 oz broccoli

2 medium carrots, peeled and sliced
vegetable stock (optional)
50 g/2 oz frozen peas
3 tablespoons baby rice

Sauté the onion in the olive oil for 2 minutes, then add all the vegetables except the frozen peas. Just cover with boiling water or vegetable stock. Bring back to the boil, then simmer for 20 minutes. Add the frozen peas and cook for 5 minutes more. Purée the vegetables, adding as much of the cooking liquid as necessary to make the desired consistency, and stir in the baby rice.

Sweet Vegetable Medley

Root vegetables like swede, carrot and parsnip make delicious and nutritious purées for young babies. Butternut squash and pumpkin can also be used to make this purée as, again, they are very popular with babies.

MAKES 5 PORTIONS

100 g/4 oz carrot, peeled and chopped
100 g/4 oz swede, peeled and chopped
100 g/4 oz potato, butternut squash or pumpkin, peeled and chopped

50 g/2 oz parsnip, peeled and chopped
300 ml/10 fl oz water or milk (can use cow's milk in cooking from 6 months)

Put the vegetables in a saucepan with the water or milk. Bring to the boil, then cover and simmer for 25–30 minutes or until the vegetables are tender. Remove with a slotted spoon and purée the vegetables in a blender, together with as much cooking liquid as necessary to make the desired consistency.

☺ ☹ ❄

Watercress, Potato and Courgette Purée

Watercress is rich in calcium and iron. It blends well with the other vegetables to make a tasty, bright green purée. You can add a little milk if your baby prefers it that way.

MAKES 12 PORTIONS

a bunch of watercress
1 large potato, peeled and chopped
350 ml / 12 fl oz vegetable stock (see page 33)

1 dessertspoon chopped parsley
75 g / 3 oz courgettes, trimmed and sliced
baby milk (optional)

Remove the leaves from the watercress and chop them into pieces. (Discard the stalks, or use them in making vegetable stock.) Put the leaves and the potato into the stock, bring to the boil and simmer for about 10 minutes. Add the parsley and courgette and simmer for another 10 minutes. Purée the mixture in a mouli and, if you like, add a little baby milk to adjust the consistency.

☺ ☹ ❄

Avocado and Papaya

This is very simple to make and the two fruits blend very well.

MAKES 1 PORTION

1 slice avocado   *1 slice papaya*

Remove the flesh from the avocado and papaya slices and mash them together until smooth. This should be eaten soon after it is made or the avocado will turn brown.

☺ | ☹

Butternut Squash and Pear

Butternut squash is one of the more unusual vegetables now available in supermarkets. It can be introduced to babies after five months; it is easily digested, rarely causes allergies, and is a good source of Vitamin A. Babies like its naturally sweet taste, which combines well with fruit; and cooking fruit and vegetables in a steamer, as here, is one of the best ways of preserving nutrients. Butternut squash is also delicious if you cut it in half, scoop out the seeds, brush each half with melted butter, and spoon 1 tablespoon of fresh orange juice into each cavity. Cover with foil and bake in the oven at 180°C (350°F) Gas 4 for 1½ hours or until tender.

MAKES 4 PORTIONS

1 medium butternut squash or pumpkin   *1 ripe juicy pear*
(about 450 g / 1 lb)

Peel the butternut squash, cut in half, remove the seeds and chop into pieces. Steam for about 12 minutes. Peel, core and chop the pear, add to the steamer and continue to cook for 5 minutes or until the squash is tender. Purée in a blender.

☺ | ☹ | ❄

Sweet Potato with Cinnamon

The addition of cinnamon gives this an extra sweetness, which babies love. This is very simple to make.

MAKES 7 PORTIONS

1 sweet potato (about 175 g / 6 oz), peeled and cut into chunks

a generous pinch of ground cinnamon
a few tablespoons baby milk

Cover the sweet potato chunks with water, bring to the boil and simmer for about 30 minutes or until soft. Drain and mash together with the cinnamon and enough baby milk to make the desired consistency.

Leek, Sweet Potato and Pea Purée

Sweet potatoes make perfect baby food; they are full of nutrients and have a naturally sweet taste and smooth texture. Choose the orange-fleshed variety as it is rich in betacarotene. It is fine to use frozen vegetables in baby purées as they are frozen within hours of being picked and can be just as nutritious as fresh vegetables. Once cooked, frozen vegetables can be re-frozen.

MAKES 5 PORTIONS

50 g / 2 oz leek, washed and sliced
400 g / 14 oz sweet potato, peeled and chopped

300 ml / 10 fl oz vegetable stock
50 g / 2 oz frozen peas

Put the leek and chopped sweet potato in a saucepan, pour over the vegetable stock and bring to the boil. Cover and simmer for 15 minutes. Add the peas and continue to cook for 5 minutes. Purée in a blender.

FOUR TO FIVE MONTH MEAL PLANNER

Week 1	Breakfast	Sleep	Lunch	Sleep*	Tea	Bedtime
Days 1–7	Breast/bottle	Breast/bottle	Breast/bottle, Baby rice	Breast/bottle	Diluted juice	Breast/bottle
Week 2						
Day 1	Breast/bottle Baby rice	Breast/bottle	Breast/bottle	Breast/bottle	Diluted juice Carrot	Breast/bottle
Day 2	Breast/bottle Baby rice	Breast/bottle	Breast/bottle	Breast/bottle	Diluted juice Carrot	Breast/bottle
Day 3	Breast/bottle Baby rice Apple	Breast/bottle	Breast/bottle	Breast/bottle	Diluted juice Carrot	Breast/bottle
Day 4	Breast/bottle Apple	Breast/bottle	Breast/bottle	Breast/bottle	Diluted juice Swede	Breast/bottle
Day 5	Breast/bottle Apple	Breast/bottle	Breast/bottle	Breast/bottle	Diluted juice Swede	Breast/bottle
Day 6	Breast/bottle Baby rice Pear	Breast/bottle	Breast/bottle	Breast/bottle	Diluted juice Potato	Breast/bottle
Day 7	Breast/bottle Pear	Breast/bottle	Breast/bottle	Breast/bottle	Diluted juice Potato	Breast/bottle

Fruit juice should be diluted at least 50/50, or substituted completely, with cooled boiled water.   *This feed is optional.

FOUR TO FIVE MONTH MEAL PLANNER

Week 3	Breakfast	Sleep	Lunch	Sleep*	Tea	Bedtime
Day 1	Breast/bottle Banana	Breast/bottle	Breast/bottle	Breast/bottle	Diluted juice or herbal tea **Sweet Vegetable Medley**	Breast/bottle
Day 2	Breast/bottle Banana	Breast/bottle	Breast/bottle	Breast/bottle	Diluted juice or herbal tea **Sweet Vegetable Medley**	Breast/bottle
Day 3	Breast/bottle **Cream of Fruit**	Breast/bottle	Breast/bottle	Breast/bottle	Diluted juice **Butternut Squash and Pear**	Breast/bottle
Day 4	Breast/bottle **Cream of Fruit**	Breast/bottle	Breast/bottle	Breast/bottle	Diluted juice **Butternut Squash and Pear**	Breast/bottle
Day 5	Breast/bottle Banana Papaya	Breast/bottle	Breast/bottle	Breast/bottle	Diluted juice **Potato, Courgette and Broccoli** Baby rice	Breast/bottle
Day 6	Breast/bottle Pear Baby rice	Breast/bottle	Breast/bottle	Breast/bottle	Diluted juice **Potato, Courgette and Broccoli** Baby rice	Breast/bottle
Day 7	Breast/bottle Pear Baby rice	Breast/bottle	Breast/bottle	Breast/bottle	Diluted juice **Carrot and Pea Purée**	Breast/bottle

Fruit juice should be diluted at least 50/50, or substituted completely, with cooled boiled water.　　　　*This feed is optional.

FOUR TO FIVE MONTH MEAL PLANNER

Week 4	Breakfast	Sleep	Lunch	Sleep*	Tea	Bedtime
Day 1	Breast/bottle **Cream of Fruit**	Breast/bottle	Breast/bottle	Breast/bottle	Diluted juice **Cream of Carrot**	Breast/bottle
Day 2	Breast/bottle **Cream of Fruit**	Breast/bottle	Breast/bottle	Breast/bottle	Diluted juice **Cream of Carrot**	Breast/bottle
Day 3	Breast/bottle **Three-Fruit Purée**	Breast/bottle	Breast/bottle	Breast/bottle	Diluted juice **Leek, Sweet Potato and Pea Purée**	Breast/bottle
Day 4	Breast/bottle **Three-Fruit Purée**	Breast/bottle	Breast/bottle	Breast/bottle	Diluted juice **Leek, Sweet Potato and Pea Purée**	Breast/bottle
Day 5	Breast/bottle Banana	Breast/bottle	Breast/bottle	Breast/bottle	Diluted juice **Broccoli Trio**	Breast/bottle
Day 6	Breast/bottle **Apple and Cinnamon**	Breast/bottle	Breast/bottle	Breast/bottle	Diluted juice **Broccoli Trio**	Breast/bottle
Day 7	Breast/bottle **Apple and Cinnamon**	Breast/bottle	Breast/bottle	Breast/bottle	Diluted juice Swede	Breast/bottle

Fruit juice should be diluted at least 50/50, or substituted completely, with cooled boiled water.   *This feed is optional.

FIVE TO SIX MONTH MEAL PLANNER

	Breakfast	*Sleep*	*Lunch*	*Sleep**	*Tea*	*Bedtime*
Day 1	Breast/bottle Baby cereal Fruit purée with milk	Breast/bottle	**Leek, Sweet Potato and Pea Purée** Diluted juice	Breast/bottle	Banana Rusk Water or diluted juice	Breast/bottle
Day 2	Breast/bottle Rusk **Apple and Raisin Compote**	Breast/bottle	Avocado Diluted juice	Breast/bottle	**Mixed Dried-Fruit Compote** Water or diluted juice	Breast/bottle
Day 3	Breast/bottle Baby cereal Peach or pear purée	Breast/bottle	**Sweet Potato with Cinnamon** Diluted juice	Breast/bottle	**Cream of Fruit** Water or diluted juice	Breast/bottle
Day 4	Breast/bottle Dried apricot and pear purée	Breast/bottle	**Baby Cereal and Vegetables** Diluted juice	Breast/bottle	Papaya Rusk Water or diluted juice	Breast/bottle
Day 5	Breast/bottle Baby cereal Papaya	Breast/bottle	Baked butternut squash Banana Diluted juice	Breast/bottle	**Avocado and Papaya** Rice cake Water or diluted juice	Breast/bottle
Day 6	Breast/bottle Baby cereal **Apple and Cinnamon**	Breast/bottle	**Potato, Courgette and Broccoli** Diluted juice	Breast/bottle	**Three-Fruit Purée** Rusk Water or diluted juice	Breast/bottle
Day 7	Breast/bottle **Mixed Dried-Fruit Compote**	Breast/bottle	**Courgette, Watercress and Potato Purée** Diluted juice	Breast/bottle	Banana Rice cake Water or diluted juice	Breast/bottle

Fruit juice should be diluted at least 50/50, or substituted completely, with cooled boiled water.   *This feed is optional.

CHAPTER THREE

SIX TO NINE MONTHS

etween six and nine months is a rapid development period for your baby. A six-month-old baby still needs to be supported whilst you are feeding him and, more often than not, still has no teeth. A nine-month-old baby, however, is usually strong enough to sit in a high chair whilst he is being fed and has already cut a few teeth. Babies of eight months are usually quite good at holding food themselves and enjoy eating small finger foods like pasta, pieces of raw or cooked vegetables or raw fruits. (Turn to pages 75–78 for suitable finger foods for young babies.) Chewing on a piece of apple will help to relieve sore gums but *never* leave your baby unattended when eating: babies have a habit of chewing up a lot of food and storing it in their mouths without swallowing and they can very easily choke. A handy tip is to give your baby some dried apple to suck. It is easy for him to hold because of the hole in the middle; it is tough to chew on so he cannot bite pieces off; and it has a lovely sweet taste. You can secure it to the high chair with a short length of string, so, if your baby drops it, it can simply be retrieved by pulling the string.

LESS MILK, MORE APPETITE

Once your baby is six months old, you can start cutting down on his milk feeds so that he is more hungry for his solids. However, he should still be taking about 600 ml/1 pint of milk per day, either as milk or in dairy products he eats. You can offer plain water or fruit juices or low-sugar herbal drinks instead of milk.

At eight or nine months, when your baby is able to hold toys fairly well himself, he is probably ready to try drinking from a cup. First try a cup with a spout, then remove the top and see how well he manages with it open. A cup with a weighted base is a good idea, so that it does not topple over and spill when your baby puts it down.

Let your baby's appetite determine how much he eats and never force him to eat something he actually dislikes. Do not offer it for a while, but reintroduce it a few weeks later. You may find that second time around he loves it.

Remember at this age it is normal for babies to be quite fat. As soon as your baby starts crawling and walking, he will lose this excess weight.

THE FOODS TO CHOOSE

Your baby can now eat protein foods like eggs, cheese, pulses, chicken and fish. Limit some foods which might be indigestible – such as spinach, lentils, cheese, berry or citrus fruit – and do not worry if some foods, like pulses, peas and raisins, pass through your child undigested: until they are about two years old, babies cannot completely digest husked vegetables and the skins of fruits. Peeling, mashing and puréeing fruit and vegetables will of course aid digestion. With foods like bread, flour, pasta and rice, try to choose wholegrain, rather than refined, as it is more nutritious.

Once your baby has passed the six-month stage and is happily eating bread and other foods containing gluten, there is no longer any need to continue giving your baby special baby cereals. You can now use adult cereals like Ready Brek, instant porridge and Weetabix, which are just as nutritious and much cheaper. Choose a cereal which is not highly refined and which is low in sugar and salt. Many people continue to use commercial baby foods because they are easy to prepare. They also think, due to the long list of vitamins and minerals on the packet, that they are more nutritious for their baby. However, babies who eat a good balanced diet of fresh foods get a perfectly adequate quantity of vitamins and minerals. Also, baby foods in general are heavily processed, and their finer texture and bland flavours will hinder the development of your baby's tastes.

Beware, too, of some of the rusks you can buy which are supposedly the 'ideal food for your baby'. They are full of sugar (some contain more sugar than a doughnut). Give your baby some toast to chew on or follow the simple recipe for rusks in the nine to twelve month finger-food section (see page 76).

Many of your own favourite recipes can be adapted for your baby once he is eight months old. When preparing a family dish, put aside the baby's portion before you add seasoning or spices and he can very often enjoy the same meal as everyone else. Many of the recipes from the previous age group's section can still be used – simply alter the texture slightly, if appropriate, and offer more.

You can now safely cook with cow's milk, although this is not suitable for milk feeds (formula or breast is better).

Fruit

There are few babies I know who do not like fruit. In the next few months, try to introduce your child to as wide a range of fruits as possible. Make fresh fruit salads with seasonal fruits chopped into little pieces and mixed with orange juice. You will find which fruits your child likes best by seeing what he leaves.

Citrus fruits, berries, dried fruits and some exotic fruits like mango can give your child an upset stomach. Limit these or you may run out of nappies! Try to remove all pith from citrus fruits to make them easier to digest.

Fresh fruits make great snacks – much better than processed, additive-laden, sugary foods, which ruin developing teeth and upset a balanced diet.

Vegetables

Once your baby starts to get teeth, you will find that he enjoys chewing slightly harder vegetables. Cut down the steaming time to preserve Vitamin C and keep them crisp. Cauliflower and broccoli florets, baby carrots and baby sweetcorn, for instance, all make excellent finger foods. Give them to your baby with his favourite vegetable purée as a dip.

Remember that, to preserve nutrients in the skin, some vegetables such as new potatoes and courgettes should not be peeled. Combinations of fruit and vegetables are popular – try squash and apple, spinach and pear, or devise your own.

Fish

Many children grow up disliking fish, which is a great shame as it is such a healthy food, full of protein and very low in fat. It is excellent for babies, easy to chew and digest, and quick to cook.

I think one of the main reasons children are put off fish is that they find it bland and boring. Counteract this with stronger tastes like cheese or tomato. If your child gets excited at the prospect of fish for dinner, then you deserve to be a very proud parent indeed.

Most paediatricians advise against fish before six months. Oily fish like salmon, tuna and sardines are particularly important for brain and visual development.

Be careful not to overcook fish, as it becomes tough and tasteless. It is cooked when the fish just flakes with a fork but is still firm. Always check very carefully for bones before serving fish.

Meat

Chicken is the first meat that should be introduced to babies. It is a great family favourite of ours, as it is very versatile and I am always concocting new ways of serving it. I was keen to get my children to like chicken from an early age so I could cook for the whole family. I have found that babies like the mild taste of chicken. It is easy and quick to cook – a great help to busy parents. Chicken blends very well with many vegetables and can have a smooth texture when puréed. Once your baby is able to handle food himself and has a few teeth, small pieces of chicken make excellent finger food and are softer and easier to chew than red meat chunks. Red meat, however, can be introduced from six months (see page 74).

Home-made chicken stock forms the basis of many recipes and I recommend that you make it in large batches. It will keep in the fridge for about 4 days and can be used to make purées.

Pasta

You will find that pasta is a great favourite with babies and mums as it is easy to chew, fun to eat and simple to cook. For babies around six months, there are very tiny pasta shapes available that are sometimes used in soups and need no chewing, or you could chop up spaghetti. Many of the vegetable purées make excellent pasta sauces, and you can always add a little grated cheese. Serve about 25 g/1 oz cooked (7–15 g/¼–½ oz dry) pasta per portion.

TEXTURES

For babies between six and eight months, the recipes should be puréed to a fairly smooth consistency. Thereafter the mixture can be coarser, with the foods mashed, finely chopped or grated, or make a gradual transition by adding grated food to a purée. Remember that foods must be soft enough for your baby's toothless gums to chew.

QUANTITIES

The portions quoted for each recipe are 50 ml/2 fl oz (about 2 ice-cube-sized portions). However, portion sizes will vary according to your baby's appetite.

FRUIT

Going Bananas

Babies love bananas and this recipe makes them taste truly scrumptious. You can also make this Jamaican-style and *flambé* the bananas with rum for a dinner party. Delicious with vanilla ice cream.

MAKES 1 PORTION

a knob of butter
1 small banana, peeled and sliced

a pinch of powdered cinnamon
2 tablespoons freshly squeezed orange juice

Melt the butter in a small frying pan, stir in the sliced banana, sprinkle with a little cinnamon and sauté for 2 minutes. Pour in the orange juice and continue to cook for another 2 minutes. Mash with a fork.

Avocado, Banana and Yoghurt

Mashed banana and avocado makes a good no-cook baby purée. Serve with or without yoghurt and eat straight away before it turns brown.

MAKES 1 PORTION

2 slices avocado
½ small banana, peeled

1 tablespoon natural Greek yoghurt

Scoop the flesh of the avocado from the skin and mash it together with the rest of the ingredients.

Peach, Apple and Strawberry Purée

This makes great baby food when sweet, juicy peaches are in season.

MAKES 4 PORTIONS

1 dessert apple, peeled, cored and chopped
1 large ripe peach, peeled, stoned and chopped

3 large strawberries, halved
1–2 tablespoons baby rice

Steam the apple for about 4 minutes. Add the peach and strawberries to the steamer and continue to cook for about 3 minutes. Blend the fruits to a smooth purée. Mix the baby rice with a tablespoon of your baby's usual milk or water and stir into the purée to thicken.

Peaches and Rice

Flaked rice is quick and easy to prepare. You could also combine the cooked rice with other fruits like nectarines or juicy plums.

MAKES 2 PORTIONS

1 tablespoon flaked rice
150 ml / 5 fl oz milk
1 ripe peach, stoned, skinned and chopped

Put the rice and milk in a small saucepan. Stir over a low heat for about 5 minutes or until it boils and thickens. Simmer for 5 minutes, then stir in the chopped peach. Purée for young babies.

Apricot, Apple and Peach Purée

Dried apricots are a concentrated source of nutrients, they are rich in iron, potassium and betacarotene, and babies tend to like their sweet flavour.

MAKES 5 PORTIONS

75 g/3 oz ready-to-eat dried apricots
2 apples, peeled, cored and chopped

1 large ripe peach, skinned, stoned and chopped, or 1 ripe pear, peeled, cored and chopped

Put the apricots into a small saucepan and cover with water. Cook over a gentle heat for 5 minutes. Add the chopped apples and continue to cook for 5 minutes. Purée together with the peach or pear.

Yoghurt and Sharon Fruit

Sharon fruit looks like an orange tomato. It must be very ripe and soft before it is eaten, and tastes a little like a sweet plum. The second portion of this recipe will keep in the fridge for the next day.

MAKES 2 PORTIONS

1 sharon fruit, or 2 slices mango or papaya

1 tablespoon Greek yoghurt

Cut the fruit in half and remove the skin. Blend or mash the flesh together with the yoghurt until smooth.

Home-Made Fruit Jelly

It's easy to make jelly with delicious fruit juices and fresh fruit. It's not full of sugar and artificial colours like some commercially made jellies.

MAKES 4 PORTIONS

600 ml/1 pint cranberry and raspberry juice
1 sachet gelatine powder

2 tablespoons caster sugar
125 g/4½ oz fresh raspberries

Place half of the juice in a small saucepan and heat until just at boiling point. Remove from the heat and stir in the gelatine and caster sugar until dissolved. If not completely dissolved, stir over a gentle heat but do not boil. Pour this into the remaining cold juice and then pour into a serving dish and stir in the raspberries. Refrigerate until set.

Blood Orange Jelly

Leaf gelatine dissolves like a dream and is fantastic for making jelly. You could also use it to make the cranberry and raspberry jelly above.

MAKES 4 PORTIONS

4 leaves gelatine
600 ml/1 pint freshly squeezed

blood orange juice
3 tablespoons caster sugar

Break the gelatine leaves into a roasting tin or shallow dish (use 6 leaves if using a mould). Pour over 6 tablespoons juice. Heat the rest of the juice until very hot but not boiling and stir in the sugar until dissolved. Remove from the heat. Little by little, take the softened gelatine out of the tin and stir into the hot juice. The gelatine will disappear. Stir in any juice left in the tin. Leave to cool. Pour the juice into a bowl, individual glasses, or jelly mould. Chill until set.

VEGETABLES
Lovely Lentils

Lentils are a good cheap source of protein. They also provide iron, which is very important for brain development particularly between the ages of six months and two years. Lentils can be difficult for young babies to digest and should be combined with plenty of fresh vegetables as in this recipe. This tasty purée also makes a delicious soup for the family by simply adding more stock and some seasoning.

MAKES 8 PORTIONS

½ small onion, finely chopped
100 g / 4 oz carrot, chopped
15 g / ½ oz celery, chopped
1 tablespoon vegetable oil
50 g / 2 oz split red lentils

200 g / 7 oz sweet potato, peeled and chopped
400 ml / 14 fl oz vegetable or chicken stock (see page 33 or 62) or water

Sauté the onion, carrot and celery in the vegetable oil for about 5 minutes or until softened. Add the lentils and sweet potato and pour over the stock or water. Bring to the boil, turn down the heat and simmer covered for 20 minutes. Purée in a blender.

Tomatoes and Carrots with Basil

If you introduce your baby to new flavours at an early age, he will tend to grow up a less fussy eater.

MAKES 4 PORTIONS

125 g/4½ oz carrots, peeled and sliced
100 g/4 oz cauliflower, cut into florets
25 g/1 oz butter
200 g/7 oz ripe tomatoes, skinned,

seeded and roughly chopped
2–3 fresh basil leaves
50 g/2 oz Cheddar cheese, grated

Put the carrots in a small saucepan, cover with boiling water and simmer, covered, for 10 minutes. Add the cauliflower and cook, covered, for 7–8 minutes, adding extra water if necessary. Meanwhile, melt the butter, add the tomatoes and sauté until mushy. Stir in the basil and cheese until melted. Purée the carrots and cauliflower with about 3 tablespoons of the cooking liquid and the tomato sauce.

Baked Sweet Potato with Orange

Sweet potatoes are delicious baked like jacket potatoes either in the oven or microwave and then combined with fruit like apple or peach purée. They are a good source of carbohydrate, vitamins and minerals.

MAKES 8 PORTIONS

1 medium sweet potato, scrubbed
2 tablespoons freshly squeezed orange juice

2 tablespoons milk

Cook the sweet potato on a baking sheet in a preheated oven at 200°C (400°F) Gas 6 for about 1 hour or until tender. Cool a little, then scoop out the flesh. Purée or mash with the orange juice and milk until smooth.

Special Spinach and Potato Purée

This purée makes a tasty introduction to spinach for your baby. It also makes a nice vegetable side dish for adults.

MAKES 7 PORTIONS

1 small onion, peeled and finely chopped
25 g / 1 oz butter
225 g / 8 oz spinach, washed, chopped and tough stalks removed

1 large or 2 small potatoes, peeled and diced
120 ml / 4 fl oz chicken stock (see page 62)

Sauté the onion in the butter over a low heat for 4–5 minutes until soft. Add the spinach and potato, pour in the stock and simmer slowly for about 35 minutes. Purée through a mouli, or mash for older babies.

Sweet Vegetable Purée

Whilst vegetables like peas and sweetcorn have a sweet taste that babies like, they should be puréed in a mouli as the husks are indigestible.

MAKES 3 PORTIONS

25 g / 1 oz chopped onion
75 g / 3 oz carrot, peeled and chopped
1 tablespoon olive oil
150 g / 5 oz potato, peeled and chopped

200 ml / 7 fl oz water
2 tablespoons frozen sweetcorn
1 tablespoon frozen peas

Fry the onion and carrot gently in the oil over for 5 minutes. Stir in the potato, add the water, bring to the boil, then cover and simmer for 10 minutes. Add the sweetcorn and peas and simmer for about 5 minutes. Purée in a mouli.

Trio of Cauliflower, Red Pepper and Sweetcorn

Babies like the bright colour and natural sweetness of these vegetables. Always purée sweetcorn in a mouli for young babies, to get rid of the tough outer skin.

MAKES 4 PORTIONS

100 g/4 oz cauliflower, broken into small florets
120 ml/4 fl oz milk

50 g/2 oz grated Cheddar cheese
25 g/1 oz red sweet pepper, chopped
75 g/3 oz frozen sweetcorn

Put the cauliflower in a small saucepan with the milk and cook over a low heat for about 8 minutes until tender. Stir in the grated cheese until melted. Meanwhile, steam the red pepper and sweetcorn or cook in some water in a small saucepan for about 6 minutes until tender.

Drain the sweetcorn and pepper. Purée together with the cauliflower milk and cheese in a mouli.

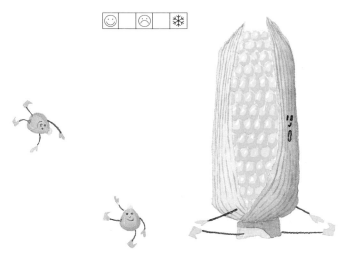

Cauliflower Cheese

This is a great favourite with babies. Try using different cheeses or combinations of cheese until you find your baby's favourite taste. The cheese sauce can be used over a mixture of vegetables as well.

MAKES 5 PORTIONS

175 g / 6 oz cauliflower

Cheese Sauce
15g / ½ oz butter
1 tablespoon plain flour
150 ml / 5 fl oz milk
50 g / 2 oz Cheddar, Edam or Gruyère
cheese, grated

Wash the cauliflower carefully, divide it into small florets and steam until tender (about 10 minutes). Meanwhile, for the sauce, melt the butter over a gentle heat in a heavy-bottomed saucepan and stir in the flour to make a smooth paste. Whisk in the milk and stir until thickened. Take the saucepan off the heat and stir in the grated cheese. Keep stirring until all the cheese has melted and the sauce is smooth.

Add the cauliflower to the sauce and purée in a blender for younger babies. For older babies, mash with a fork or chop into little pieces.

Courgette Gratin

This creamy purée is also good using broccoli.

MAKES 6 PORTIONS

1 medium potato (about 100g/4 oz), peeled and chopped
175 g/6 oz courgettes, sliced

a knob of butter
40 g/1½ oz Cheddar or Gruyère cheese
4 tablespoons milk

Boil the potato until soft. Steam the courgettes for 8 minutes. Drain the potatoes, add the butter and cheese and stir until melted. Purée the potato mixture, courgettes and milk with an electric hand blender.

Leek and Potato with Fromage Frais

This was Lara's favourite vegetable purée. It also makes a superb vegetable soup for adults.

MAKES 8 PORTIONS

25 g/1 oz margarine or 2 tablespoons oil
175 g/6 oz leeks, carefully washed and sliced
225 g/8 oz potatoes, peeled and diced

450 ml/15 fl oz chicken stock (see page 62)
2 tablespoons fromage frais

Heat the margarine in a heavy-based pan. Add the leeks and cook over a gentle heat for 10 minutes until softened, stirring occasionally. Add the diced potatoes and stock and simmer, covered, for 25–30 minutes until tender. Purée and stir in the fromage frais.

Courgette and Pea Souper

When I experimented with this combination, the baby purée turned out to be so good that I also made a delicious soup for the rest of the family. Simply increase the quantities and add extra stock and seasoning.

MAKES 4 PORTIONS

½ small onion, peeled and finely chopped
15 g/½ oz butter or margarine
50 g/2 oz courgette, trimmed and thinly sliced

1 medium potato (about 150 g/5 oz), peeled and chopped
120 ml/4 fl oz chicken or vegetable stock (see page 62 or 33)
25 g/1 oz frozen peas

Sauté the onion in the butter or margarine until softened. Add the courgette, potato and stock. Bring to the boil, then cover and simmer for 12 minutes. Add the frozen peas, bring to the boil, then reduce the heat and continue to cook for 5 minutes. Purée in a blender.

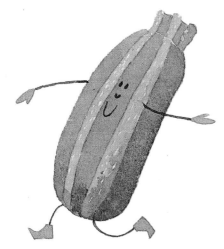

Minestrone

The vegetables in minestrone soup add texture but are nice and soft for your baby to chew. However, for younger babies you could blend this soup to the desired texture. Add a little seasoning and some extra stock to make this into a delicious soup for the rest of the family.

MAKES 4 ADULT PORTIONS OR 12 BABY PORTIONS

1 tablespoon vegetable oil
½ small onion, finely chopped
½ leek, white part only, washed and finely chopped
1 medium carrot, peeled and diced
½ celery stick, diced
100 g/4 oz French beans, cut into 1 cm/½ inch lengths

1 potato, peeled and diced
1 tablespoon finely chopped parsley
2 teaspoons tomato purée
1.2 litres/2 pints chicken or vegetable stock (see pages 62 and 33)
3 tablespoons frozen peas
50 g/2 oz very small pasta shapes

Heat the oil in a saucepan and fry the onion and leek for 2 minutes, then add the carrot, celery, French beans, potato and parsley and sauté for 4 minutes. Stir in the tomato purée and cook for 1 minute. Pour over the chicken or vegetable stock and simmer, covered, for 20 minutes. Add the frozen peas and pasta and cook for 5 minutes (check the packet instructions for the cooking time of pasta).

FISH

Plaice with Tomatoes and Potato

This makes a good, creamy-textured fish purée.

MAKES 4 PORTIONS

1 fillet of plaice, skinned
2 medium tomatoes, skinned, seeded and
chopped
a little margarine or butter

1 bay leaf
150 ml/5 fl oz milk
1 small potato, peeled

Put the plaice into a dish, cover with the chopped tomato, dot with a little margarine or butter and add the bay leaf. Pour over most of the milk. Cover with foil and cook in an oven preheated to 180°C (350°F) Gas 4, for 20 minutes. (Alternatively, cover with a lid and cook in the microwave on High for about 3 minutes.)

Whilst the fish is cooking, boil the potato. When soft, mash it with the remaining milk and margarine or butter. Flake the fish when it is cooked, remove the bay leaf and mash or purée the fish together with the liquid in which it was cooked. You can either mix in the mashed potato or serve it as an accompaniment to the fish.

Fillets of Fish in Cheese Sauce

Fish and cheese sauce go really well together and the combination is always popular. Add some chives and you give an old recipe a new taste.

MAKES 6 PORTIONS

175 g/6 oz cod, plaice or hake, filleted
and skinned
3 tablespoons milk
1 bay leaf
a knob of butter

Cheese Sauce
20 g/¾ oz butter
2 tablespoons plain flour
175 ml/6 fl oz milk
65 g/2½ oz Cheddar cheese, grated
1 teaspoon chopped parsley or
snipped chives

Put the fish in a suitable dish together with the milk and bay leaf and dot with butter. Cover and microwave on High for about 4 minutes. Alternatively, poach the fish in milk in a saucepan until cooked.

To prepare the sauce, melt the butter and stir in the flour to make a roux. Gradually whisk in the milk, cooking over a gentle heat until you have a smooth white sauce. Allow the sauce to come to the boil and simmer for 1 minute, stirring constantly. Take the saucepan off the heat and whisk in the cheese until melted. Add the parsley or snipped chives.

Flake the fish with a fork, checking to make sure there are no stray bones. Mix together the flaked fish and cheese sauce and mash or purée in a blender.

☺ ☹ ❄

Plaice with Spinach and Cheese

Frozen vegetables are a good alternative to fresh, and can often be more nutritious than vegetables that have been in the kitchen for several days. It also means you can make this when fresh spinach is not available.

MAKES 8 PORTIONS

225 g/8 oz plaice fillets, skinned
1 tablespoon milk
1 bay leaf
a few peppercorns
a knob of butter
175 g/6 oz fresh or 75 g/3 oz frozen spinach

Cheese Sauce
25 g/1 oz butter
2 tablespoons plain flour
175 ml/6 fl oz milk
50 g/2 oz Gruyère cheese

Put the plaice in a suitable dish with the milk, bay leaf, peppercorns and butter. Microwave for about 3 minutes on High or poach in a saucepan for 5 minutes. Meanwhile, cook the spinach in a saucepan with just a little water clinging to the leaves for about 3 minutes or cook frozen spinach following the package directions. Squeeze out the excess water. Make the cheese sauce (see page 59). Discard the bay leaf and peppercorns, flake the fish carefully and purée with the spinach and cheese sauce to the desired consistency.

☺ ☹ ❄

Fillet of Cod with Sweet Potato

The orange-fleshed sweet potato is an excellent source of betacarotene, which may help to prevent certain types of cancer. Babies tend to love the taste of sweet potato, so this recipe makes a good introduction to fish.

MAKES 8 PORTIONS

225 g/8 oz sweet potato, peeled
75 g/3 oz cod, skinned and filleted
2 tablespoons milk

a knob of butter
juice of 1 orange (about 120 ml/4 fl oz)

Put the sweet potato into a saucepan, just cover with water, bring to the boil, then cover and simmer for 20 minutes or until soft. Put the fish in a suitable dish, add the milk, dot with butter, cover and microwave on High for 2 minutes or until the fish is cooked. Alternatively, poach the fish in a saucepan with the milk and butter for 6–7 minutes or until just cooked through. Put the cooked sweet potato, drained fish and orange juice into a blender and purée until smooth.

Fillet of Fish in an Orange Sauce

This is one of my family's favourite fish recipes. Do not be put off by the odd combination, as it gives a marvellous rich taste.

MAKES 5 PORTIONS

225 g/8 oz fillet of fish, skinned, e.g.
cod, haddock or hake
juice of 1 orange (about 120 ml/4 fl oz)
40 g/1½ oz Cheddar cheese, grated

1 dessertspoon finely chopped parsley
25 g/1 oz crushed cornflakes
7 g/¼ oz margarine

Put the haddock in a greased dish, cover with the orange juice, cheese, parsley and cornflakes and dot with the margarine. Cover with foil and bake at 180°C (350°F) Gas 4 for about 20 minutes. Alternatively, cover with a lid and cook in a microwave on High for 4 minutes.

Flake the fish carefully, removing any bones, and mash everything together with the liquid in which the fish was cooked.

CHICKEN

Chicken Stock and My First Chicken Purée

Recipes taste much better if you use home-made chicken stock. I make it in large batches, divide it up into small containers, keep it in the freezer and use it as a base for soups, and chicken and vegetable purées. For babies over one year, you can add 2 or 3 chicken stock cubes to the recipe for a stronger flavour.

MAKES APPROXIMATELY 2.25 LITRES/4 PINTS

1 large boiler chicken, plus giblets
2 parsnips
3 carrots
2 leeks

2 large onions
1 celery stalk
3 sprigs of fresh parsley

Cut the chicken into eight pieces, trimming excess fat. Trim, peel and wash the vegetables as necessary. Put the chicken pieces into a large saucepan together with the giblets. Cover with 2.25 litres/4 pints water, bring to the boil and skim the froth from the top. Add the vegetables and parsley and simmer for about 3 hours. It is best to remove the chicken breasts after about 1½ hours if you are going to eat them; otherwise they will become too dry.

Leave the soup in the fridge overnight and remove any congealed fat from the top in the morning. Strain out all the chicken and vegetables to make the chicken stock. Season to taste.

You can purée some of the chicken breast in a mouli, together with a selection of the vegetables and some stock to make a chicken and vegetable purée for your baby, or purée the vegetables and stock for a non-clear soup for adults!

Chicken with Cottage Cheese

Babies of this age are a little too young to eat pieces of chicken as finger food. This and the following three recipes show you simple ways of transforming cold chicken into tasty food for your baby.

MAKES 2 PORTIONS

50 g/2 oz cooked boneless chicken, chopped
1 tablespoon natural yoghurt

1½ tablespoons cottage cheese with pineapple

Mix together the chicken, yoghurt and cottage cheese. Blend to the desired consistency.

☺ ☹

Chicken with Parsnip and Beans

If freezing this recipe, do not purée the chicken with the vegetables until they are cold. It is important to avoid warming the chicken.

MAKES 5 PORTIONS

50 g/2 oz parsnip, trimmed, peeled and sliced
100 g/4 oz potato, peeled and chopped

25 g/1 oz green beans, topped and tailed
40 g/1½ oz cooked boneless chicken
4 tablespoons milk

Put the vegetables into a saucepan, cover with water, bring to the boil, then cover and simmer until they are tender. Drain the vegetables and purée, together with the cooked chicken and milk.

☺ ☹ ❄

Chicken with Potato and Tomato

As with the previous recipe, avoid warming the chicken if you are going to freeze this.

MAKES 3 PORTIONS

1 medium potato, peeled
2 tablespoons milk
1 medium tomato, skinned and seeded

50 g/2 oz cooked boneless chicken, chopped

Boil the potato until soft. Mash the potato with the milk and the tomato flesh, then add the chicken. Make into a purée in the blender. (If too thick, add a little extra milk.)

Chicken Salad Purée

What could be simpler? For toddlers, simply chop the ingredients, leave out the yoghurt and mix with mayonnaise or salad cream.

MAKES 1 PORTION

25 g/1 oz cooked boneless chicken
1 slice cucumber, peeled and chopped
1 small tomato, skinned, seeded and chopped
50 g/2 oz avocado, peeled and chopped
1 tablespoon mild natural yoghurt

Put all the ingredients into a blender and purée until the desired consistency. Serve immediately.

Chicken in Tomato Sauce

MAKES 12 PORTIONS

25 g/1 oz chopped onion
100 g/4 oz carrot, thinly sliced
1½ tablespoons vegetable oil
1 small chicken breast, cut into chunks

100 g/4 oz potato, peeled and chopped
200 g/7 oz canned chopped tomatoes
150 ml/5 fl oz chicken stock

Sauté the onion and carrot in the vegetable oil until softened, then add the chicken and potato and continue to cook for 3 minutes. Pour over the chopped tomatoes together with the chicken stock. Bring to the boil and cook over a gentle heat for about 30 minutes or until the potato is quite soft. Put the mixture through a mouli or, for babies of nine months and older, chop in a blender. You could also add a little milk to make a smoother texture if you wish.

Easy One-Pot Chicken

This is an ideal purée for introducing young babies to chicken.

MAKES 12 PORTIONS

½ small onion, peeled and chopped
15 g/½ oz butter
100 g/4 oz chicken breast, cut into chunks
1 medium carrot, peeled and sliced

275 g/10 oz sweet potato, peeled and chopped
300 ml/10 fl oz chicken stock (see page 62)

Sauté the onion in the butter until softened. Add the chicken breast and sauté for 3–4 minutes. Add the vegetables, pour over the stock, bring to the boil and simmer, covered, for about 30 minutes or until the chicken is cooked through and the vegetables are tender. Purée in a blender to the desired consistency.

Chicken with Grapes and Courgette

The addition of grapes to this recipe gives the chicken a little sweetness, which babies love. It is very simple to make and is usually gobbled up pretty quickly.

MAKES 4 PORTIONS

1 chicken breast or 2 chicken thighs, skinned and off the bone
150 ml/5 fl oz chicken stock (see page 62)

8 white grapes, peeled and seeded
1 courgette, trimmed and sliced
1 tablespoon baby rice

Cut the chicken into small pieces. Put all the ingredients except the baby rice into a small saucepan, bring to the boil and simmer for 10 minutes. Purée to the desired consistency and thicken by stirring in the baby rice.

☺ ☹

RED MEATS

Braised Beef with Sweet Potato

Both this and the recipe below make good introductions to red meat.

MAKES 6 PORTIONS

1 leek, washed and sliced
20 g/¾ oz butter
100 g/4 oz braising steak or lamb, cut
into cubes
2 tablespoons flour

275 g/10 oz sweet potato, peeled and
chopped
300 ml/10 fl oz chicken stock (see
page 62)
juice of 1 orange (about 120 ml/4 fl oz)

In a flameproof casserole, soften the leek in the butter. Roll the meat in the flour and add to the leek to brown. Add the sweet potato, stock and orange juice. Bring to the boil, cover and transfer to an oven preheated to 180°C (350°F) Gas 4 for 1¼ hours or until the meat is tender. Blend to the desired consistency.

☺ ☹ ❄

Liver Special

MAKES 6 PORTIONS

75 g/3 oz calf's liver, or 2 chicken livers
120 ml/4 fl oz chicken stock (see page 62)
25 g/1 oz leek, white part only, chopped
25 g/1 oz mushrooms, chopped

50 g/2 oz carrot, chopped
1 potato, peeled and chopped
a knob of butter
½ tablespoon milk

Trim and chop the liver and cook in the stock with the leek, mushrooms and carrot for about 8 minutes over a low heat. Boil the potato until tender and mash with the butter and milk. Purée the liver and vegetables and mix with the potato.

☺ ☹ ❄

PASTA

Tomato and Courgette Pasta Stars

This tasty pasta sauce takes only about 10 minutes to prepare.

MAKES 3 PORTIONS

25 g / 1 oz pasta stars, uncooked
75 g / 3 oz courgette, trimmed and diced
25 g / 1 oz butter

3 medium tomatoes (about 200 g / 7 oz), skinned, seeded and chopped
25 g / 1 oz Cheddar cheese, grated

Cook the pasta according to the packet instructions, or longer for young babies. Sauté the courgette in the butter for about 5 minutes. Add the tomatoes and cook over a gentle heat for 5 minutes. Remove from the heat and stir in the cheese until melted. Purée in a blender and stir in the pasta.

Mushroom Pasta Sauce

MAKES 2 PORTIONS OF SAUCE

1 tablespoon olive oil
25 g / 1 oz chopped onion
½ garlic clove, peeled and crushed

40 g / 1½ oz sliced button mushrooms
65 g / 2½ oz peeled and chopped potato
100 ml / 3½ fl oz milk
100 ml / 3½ fl oz water

Heat the oil and sauté the onion and garlic for 1 minute. Add the mushrooms and sauté for 3 minutes. Add the potato, milk and water and bring to the boil. Cover and simmer for 10 minutes. Purée in a mouli or blender, add a little extra milk if necessary and serve with tiny pasta shapes.

My First Bolognese Sauce

A tasty recipe to encourage your baby to enjoy eating red meat.

MAKES 5 PORTIONS

1 tablespoon olive oil
1 small onion, peeled and chopped
1 medium carrot, peeled and grated
½ celery stick, finely chopped
100 g / 4 oz lean minced beef

3 medium tomatoes, skinned and chopped
½ teaspoon tomato purée
150 ml / 5 fl oz unsalted chicken stock
3 tablespoons tiny pasta shapes

Heat the oil and fry the onion, carrot and celery over a medium heat for about 4 minutes. Add the minced beef and fry until browned, stirring occasionally. Stir in the tomatoes, tomato purée and chicken stock. Bring to the boil, then simmer for 15 minutes. Meanwhile, cook the pasta shapes according to the packet directions. Transfer the sauce to a blender and purée to a fairly smooth consistency. Drain the pasta and mix with the sauce.

Tomato and Basil Pasta Sauce

Butterfly-shaped pasta is fun for babies to grasp in their hands.

MAKES 2 PORTIONS OF SAUCE

15 g / ½ oz butter
2 tablespoons chopped onion
150 g / 5 oz ripe tomatoes, skinned,

seeded and chopped
2 torn basil leaves
2 teaspoons cream cheese

Melt the butter in a pan and sauté the onion until softened. Add the tomatoes and sauté for 3 minutes or until mushy. Stir in the basil and cream cheese and heat through. Purée in a blender.

Napolitana Pasta Sauce

A tasty tomato sauce which goes well with all types of pasta – my
children love this with ravioli stuffed with ricotta and spinach.

MAKES 4 PORTIONS OF SAUCE

1 tablespoon olive oil
½ small onion, peeled and chopped
½ garlic clove, peeled and crushed
50 g/2 oz carrot, peeled and chopped
200 ml/7 fl oz passata

3 tablespoons water
2 basil leaves, roughly torn
1 teaspoon grated Parmesan cheese
1 teaspoon cream cheese

Heat the olive oil and sauté the onion, garlic and carrot for 6 minutes.
Add the passata, water, basil and Parmesan. Cover and simmer for
15 minutes. Purée the sauce and stir in the cream cheese. Mix with pasta
and serve.

Popeye Pasta

MAKES 8 PORTIONS

100 g/4 oz frozen or 225 g/8 oz fresh
spinach, washed
50 g/2 oz tiny pasta shapes (like soup
pasta), uncooked

15 g/½ oz butter
2 tablespoons milk
2 tablespoons cream cheese
40 g/1½ oz Gruyère cheese, grated

Cook the spinach following package directions or, if fresh, with just the
water clinging to its leaves in a microwave or in a saucepan over a low
heat until tender. Press out the excess water. Cook the pasta according to
the packet instructions. Meanwhile, melt the butter in a small frying pan
and sauté the cooked spinach. Combine the spinach with the milk and
cheeses, and chop finely in a food processor. Mix with the cooked pasta.

SIX TO NINE MONTH MEAL PLANNER

	Breakfast	Sleep	Lunch	Sleep	Tea	Bedtime
Day 1	Weetabix with milk Mashed banana	Milk	**My First Chicken Purée** Grated apple Juice	Milk	**Leek and Potato with Fromage Frais** Pear purée Water or juice	Milk
Day 2	Ready Brek or porridge with milk Fruit purée Milk	Milk	**Plaice with Tomatoes and Potato** Mashed banana Juice	Milk	**Courgette and Pea Souper** Yoghurt Water or juice	Milk
Day 3	**Apple and Baby Cereal** Toast Milk	Milk	**Cauliflower Cheese** Grated pear Juice	Milk	**Braised Beef with Sweet Potato** Rusk Water or juice	Milk
Day 4	Baby cereal with milk Dried apricot purée Fromage frais	Milk	**Lovely Lentils Peaches and Rice** Juice	Milk	**Minestrone** Toast Water or juice	Milk
Day 5	Weetabix with milk **Peaches, Apples and Pears**	Milk	Pasta with **Mushroom Pasta Sauce Going Bananas** Milk	Milk	**My First Bolognese Sauce** Pear purée Water or juice	Milk
Day 6	Baby cereal with milk **Yoghurt and Sharon Fruit**	Milk	**Courgette Gratin Home-Made Fruit Jelly** Milk	Milk	**Fillet of Fish in an Orange Sauce** Apple Water	Milk
Day 7	Ready Brek with milk **Yoghurt and Sharon Fruit**	Milk	**Special Spinach and Potato Purée Apricot, Apple and Peach Purée** Juice	Milk	**Easy One-Pot Chicken** Papaya purée Water or juice	Milk

CHAPTER FOUR

NINE TO TWELVE MONTHS

Towards the end of the first year, a baby's weight gain usually slows down quite dramatically. Often babies who have been good eaters in the past become much more difficult to feed. Many refuse to be spoon-fed and want to assert their new-found independence, using their hands to feed themselves. My older daughter at the age of ten months went through a phase of refusing to eat anything offered to her on a spoon. I was determined that she should eat the home-made purées I had prepared, so I gave her various finger foods like steamed carrots or strips of toast, which I dipped into the purées. That way I succeeded in getting her to eat and enjoy them, and everyone was happy.

MEALTIME PATIENCE

Let your baby experiment by allowing her to use a spoon. Most of the food will probably end up on you or on the floor, but with practice your baby's aim will get better! Put a waterproof tablecloth under the high chair to catch the food that falls on the floor. It is probably best to have two bowls of food and two spoons; one which you use to spoon-feed your baby, the other (preferably a bowl which sticks to the table by suction) for your baby to play with. You will need lots of patience at mealtimes, as many babies are very easily distracted at this stage and prefer to play with their food rather than eat it. If all else fails, I find that if you can attract their attention by giving them a small toy to hold, you can sometimes slip food into their mouths on a spoon and they will eat without really noticing what they are doing and forget to put up any resistance!

No child under the age of one year needs to drink cow's milk. For drinks, continue using formula or breast milk, which has a much lower salt content and is complete with essential vitamins. However, as solid-food intake increases, milk need no longer form such a staple part of your child's diet, although they should still be drinking about 600 ml/1 pint of milk a day (or the equivalent as dairy products or in cooking). It is an important source of protein and calcium. Many mothers assume that when their baby cries it is because she wants more milk, but often babies of this age are given *too much* milk and not enough solid food. If you fill your baby's stomach with milk when she really wants some solid food, you will not get a very satisfied baby.

If you have a juice extractor, you can make all sorts of wonderful fruit and vegetable drinks for your baby – try combinations like apple and banana juice. Your baby should now be drinking happily from a cup, the bottle kept for her bedtime drink of warm milk.

Your baby will be teething at this age and very often sore gums can put her off eating for a while. Don't worry, as she will make up for this later that day or the next day. (Rubbing a teething gel on your baby's gums, or giving her something very cold to chew, can help relieve soreness and restore appetite.)

It is a good idea to eat something with your baby at mealtimes. There are some mothers who sit opposite their babies and try to spoon food into their mouths whilst eating nothing themselves. Babies are great mimics and will be more likely to enjoy eating if they see you tucking in as well.

THE FOODS TO CHOOSE

Now you can be a little more adventurous with the food that you make for your baby. It is a good idea to develop her tastes for garlic and herbs, both of which are very healthy. Children tend to be less fussy eaters if they are introduced to a wide range of foods early. Again, if your baby dislikes certain foods, never force her to eat them; just leave out those foods and perhaps reintroduce them in a couple of months' time. Try also to vary the foods as much as possible, as this will lead to a more balanced diet. If you give your child a favourite food too often, it is possible she will go off it altogether.

Your baby can now eat berry fruits (but these should still be put through a mouli in the earlier stages to get rid of the indigestible seeds). Fruit jellies will be interesting for your baby to look at, feel and eat. Your baby will like fruit and vegetables that have been grated.

Oily fish can now be introduced; it contains iron and fat-soluble vitamins, which white fish does not. All fish must obviously be very fresh. Chicken dishes can become more interesting in both texture and tastes and the types of pasta cooked can be large enough for the independent baby to pick up (butterflies, spirals, shells and animal shapes are good). Increase the quantity per serving of pasta to about 40 g/$1\frac{1}{2}$ oz cooked (15–20 g/$\frac{1}{2}$–$\frac{3}{4}$ oz dry).

Whenever possible, try to make the food look attractive on the plate. Choose contrasting colours and arrange the food in pretty shapes. You can use your imagination to make little faces or animals. Never pile too much food on to the plate but give a second helping – your baby will let you know in no uncertain terms if she wants more.

Meat

Babies are born with a store of iron which lasts for about six months. Red meat is the best source of iron, and a baby's requirements are particularly high between six and twelve months. A good meat to introduce is liver; it is the richest natural source of iron and is easily digested. Much to our surprise, our children enjoy liver (neither my husband nor I can bear the taste)!

Red meat cooked off the bone should be quite safe to give to babies provided it is bought from a reputable source. If using minced meat, choose some good-quality meat and ask your butcher to mince it for you rather than buy it ready-prepared. Do not give sausages or other processed meats to children, like pâté or meat pies. After cooking minced meat for young babies, I find that if I chop it in a food processor for 30 seconds, it becomes softer and easier to chew – it is often the texture of meat rather than the taste that puts children off.

TEXTURES AND QUANTITIES

It is easy to get into the habit of only giving your baby soft foods, but you should try to vary the consistency of food that you give your baby. There is no need to purée all foods. Babies do not need teeth to be able to chew; gums do a great job on foods that are not too hard. Give some food mashed (fish), some grated (cheese), some diced (carrots) and some whole (pieces of chicken, slices of toast and pieces of raw fruit).

As far as quantities are concerned, you must let your baby's appetite be your guide. The portions in the recipes are a guide to what an average baby of this age would eat (two to three ice-cube-sized blocks, no longer singles). You could start to freeze food in larger containers, like empty yoghurt pots, well covered with foil or polythene bags. Many meals in this chapter can be enjoyed by the whole family, in which case adult-sized portions are given.

FINGER FOODS

By nine months, your baby will probably want to start feeding herself. It is a good idea, therefore, to start giving her some foods that are easy to eat with her fingers. Finger foods are great for occupying your child while you prepare her meal – or you could make a whole meal of finger foods.

Never leave your child unattended whilst eating. It is very easy for a baby to choke on even very small pieces of food. Avoid giving your baby whole nuts, fruits with stones, whole grapes, ice cubes, olives and any other foods that might get stuck in her throat.

Raw Fruit

When giving fruit, make sure any pips or stones have been removed. If your baby finds it difficult to chew, give soft fruits that melt in the mouth – bananas, peaches or grated fruits. Berry and citrus fruits should only be given in small quantities to start with. Remove as much pith as possible.

Many babies who are teething really enjoy biting into fruit. A banana put into the freezer for a few hours makes an excellent teething aid for young babies. Once your baby is able to hold food successfully, give her larger pieces of fruit and encourage her to bite little bits off. (But don't let her *store* these in her mouth; on occasion I had to resort to opening my son's mouth and removing food he refused to swallow!) If your baby has only a few teeth, then it is a good idea to give her grated fruit.

FRUITY IDEAS

apple, apricots, avocado, banana, blueberries, cherries, clementine, grapes, kiwi fruit, mango, melon, nectarine, orange, papaya, peach, pear, plum, raspberries, strawberries, tomato

---

Dried Fruits

These are a good source of fibre, iron and energy. Choose ready-to-eat ones which are soft. Some dried apricots are treated with suphur dioxide to preserve their bright orange colour; avoid these as they can trigger an asthma attack in susceptible babies. Don't give lots of dried fruit as it can be difficult to digest – and laxative.

MORE FRUITY IDEAS

apple rings, apricots, banana chips, dates, peaches, pears, prunes, raisins, sultanas

---

Vegetables

To begin with, give your baby soft cooked vegetables cut into pieces that are easy for her to hold, and encourage her to bite off little pieces. (It is best to steam vegetables as this will help to preserve Vitamin C.) Gradually cook the vegetables for less time so that your baby gets used to having to chew harder. Once your baby has good coordination, she will enjoy picking up little vegetables like peas and sweetcorn.

Once your baby has mastered the art of feeding herself cooked vegetables, you can introduce carefully washed grated raw vegetables and sticks of raw vegetables. Even if your baby is unable to bite into these sticks, she will enjoy chewing on them as an aid to teething. In fact, sticks of raw vegetables such as carrots and cucumber are very soothing for sore gums if they are chilled in the freezer or in iced water for a few minutes. Large pieces of raw vegetables are safer than small pieces as a baby will nibble off what she can manage, whereas a small piece put into her mouth whole could cause her to choke if she tried to swallow it.

Once your baby can chew well, try giving her corn on the cob. Cut the corn in half or into three pieces or look out for little mini-sized corn cobs in some supermarkets – just right for babies. Corn is fun to eat and babies love to hold and chew it.

Vegetables are also very good dipped into sauces and purées. Try using some of the recipes for vegetable purées as dipping sauces.

VEGETABLE VARIETY

aubergine, beans (green), broccoli, Brussels sprouts, cabbage, carrots, cauliflower, celery, courgettes, mangetout, mushrooms, peas, potato, swede, sweetcorn (including corn on the cob and baby corn), sweet pepper, sweet potato

---

Breads and Rusks

Pieces of toast, rusks and firm bread, like pitta bread, can be dipped into purées and sauces. Often a baby who refuses to be spoon-fed will eat her meal by sucking it off a rusk or a piece of toast.

Many baby rusks on the market contain as much sugar as a sweet biscuit and even so-called low-sugar rusks can contain more than 15 per cent sugar. It is very easy to make your own sugar-free alternative from wholemeal bread.

HOME-MADE RUSKS

For home-made savoury rusks, simply cut a thick (1 cm/½ inch) slice of wholemeal (granary or rye) bread into three strips. Melt ⅛ teaspoon Marmite in 1 teaspoon boiling water, and brush this evenly over the bread strips. Bake in the oven preheated to 180°C (350°F) Gas 4 for 15 minutes. Leave out the Marmite if your baby prefers and add a little grated cheese. You can prepare a store of rusks in advance and keep them in an airtight container for 3–4 days.

Rice cakes come in all different flavours and are excellent for teething, as they seem to hold together well.

Miniature Sandwiches

Little sandwiches cut into fingers, squares, small triangles or even animal shapes using a biscuit cutter are very popular with babies. Some suggestions for sandwich fillings are given below; see also the toddler section for a more exhaustive list (pages 186–187).

FILLING SUGGESTIONS

mashed banana, avocado and chopped tomato, chopped chicken with fruit chutney, cottage cheese and grated apple, cream cheese and strawberry jam, Marmite and grated cheese, cheese, tomato and grated cucumber, mashed sardines with tomato ketchup

---

Breakfast Cereals

Babies love to pick up and eat little pieces of breakfast cereal. Try to choose cereals that are fortified with iron and vitamins and which do not have added sugar. Again, some suggestions are given below.

GOOD MORNING MUNCHIES

Cheerios, cornflakes, Granola, Shreddies

Cheese

Start by giving your baby grated cheese or cut wafer-thin slices. Once she has mastered chewing, you can move on to chunks and strips of cheese. I have found that the following cheeses are especially popular: Cheddar, mozzarella, Edam, Gouda, Emmenthal and Gruyère. Cream cheese and cottage cheeses are also favourites. Keep away from strong cheeses like blue cheese, Brie and Camembert. Always make sure that the cheese you give your baby is pasteurised.

Pasta

Pasta comes in all shapes and sizes, it is soft to chew and is very appealing to babies. I have given some recipes for pasta sauces but most of the vegetable purées can also be served with pasta. You can try tossing pasta in melted butter and sprinkling with grated cheese. My children enjoy eating spaghetti as finger food!

Meat

Slices or chunks of cooked chicken (or turkey) make great finger food. As well as plain pieces of chicken, try giving your baby chicken cooked in a sauce. Very often the sauce makes the chicken more tender and so it is easier for your baby to chew.

Miniature chicken balls are another favourite (try my recipe for Chicken and Apple Balls, page 98). Your baby may also enjoy chewing on miniature drumsticks. Remove the skin and make sure that your baby avoids eating any pieces of bone. There is a fine needle-like bone in all drumsticks that is potentially very dangerous – extra care needs to be taken.

Strips of sautéed liver make good finger food as they are easy to hold and soft to eat. Try, too, some miniature meatballs (see page 154). Pieces of steak and chunks of meat are generally too tough for young babies to chew.

Fish

Pieces of flaked white fish are good as they are low in fat, high in protein and easy for your child to chew. You can give them to your baby either plain or mixed with a sauce. Do take extra care when serving fish to your baby in any recipe to check the fish thoroughly for bones before you cook it and when flaking it.

Make your own fish fingers, fish balls and fish cakes (see pages 94, 133–134).

BREAKFAST

The first meal of the day is important for all of us after a night's fasting, particularly so for energetic babies and toddlers!

Recipes can now contain more interesting and more nutritious grains. Wheatgerm is particularly good and can be sprinkled on to cereals or yoghurt. Mixing cereals and fruit makes a delicious and nutritious start to the day. Many of the home-made cereals can be mixed with apple juice instead of milk.

Cheese is important for strong bones and teeth. You can offer cheese on toast or little strips for your baby to hold. Eggs are an excellent source of protein, vitamins and iron. Give your baby scrambled eggs or an omelette but make sure that the white and yolk are cooked until solid. Fresh fruit provides vitamins, minerals and substances called phytochemicals which help prevent cancer. Give fruit as finger foods, make fruit salads or offer stewed fruit, such as apple or rhubarb.

Highly refined, sugar-coated cereals should be avoided. Do not be fooled by the list of added vitamins on the side of the packet – unprocessed cereals are much healthier for your child.

There are also some recipes in the toddler baking and fruit dessert sections that make excellent breakfast food: Pineapple and Raisin Muffins (page 175), Funny Shape Biscuits (page 172) or Snow-Covered Fruit Salad (page 165).

BREAKFAST
Fruity Swiss Muesli

This tasty and nutritious breakfast will make a good start to the day for the whole family. You can vary the fruit in the muesli, adding, for example, peaches, strawberries, bananas or ready-to-eat apricots.

MAKES 4 CHILD OR 2 ADULT PORTIONS

65 g/2½ oz rolled oats
15 g/½ oz wheat germ
175 ml/6 fl oz apple juice
1 teaspoon lemon juice

1 apple, peeled and grated
1 pear, peeled, cored and chopped
1 tablespoon maple syrup
120–150 ml/4–5 fl oz natural yoghurt

Combine the rolled oats, wheat germ and apple juice. Set aside for a couple of hours or refrigerate overnight. Next morning, mix the lemon juice with the grated apple and stir this into the oat mixture together with the chopped pear, maple syrup and yoghurt.

Fruity Yoghurt

Many commercial fruit yoghurts have a lot of added sugar. It is easy to make your own, adding a combination of your baby's favourite foods.

MAKES 2 PORTIONS

½ ripe peach stoned, skinned and chopped
½ small banana, peeled and chopped

150 ml / 5 fl oz natural yoghurt
2 teaspoons maple syrup

Simply mix all the ingredients together and serve. Mash the fruit for younger babies.

Banana and Prune Fool

This only takes a couple of minutes to prepare and it is very tasty. It is also a good recipe to try if your baby is a little bit constipated.

MAKES 1 PORTION

5 canned prunes in fruit juice, stoned
1 small ripe banana, peeled

1 tablespoon natural yoghurt
1 tablespoon cream cheese

Whiz the prunes, banana, yoghurt and cream cheese together in a blender with 1–2 tablespoons of the juice from the canned fruit.

Apricot, Apple and Pear Custard

Dried apricots are one of nature's great health foods. They are a good concentrated source of betacarotene, potassium and iron. This tasty fruit purée works well for breakfast or dessert.

MAKES 3 PORTIONS

75 g/3 oz ready-to-eat dried apricots
1 large eating apple, peeled, cored and chopped

1 tablespoon custard powder
150 ml/5 fl oz milk
1 ripe pear, peeled, cored and chopped

Gently heat the apricots and apple in a small saucepan with 4 table-spoons water for 8–10 minutes or until soft. In a saucepan, blend the custard powder with a little of the milk to make a smooth paste. Then add the remaining milk and slowly bring to the boil, stirring until thickened and smooth. Blend the cooked fruit and pear to the desired consistency and stir in the custard.

☺ ☹ ❄

A Grown-Up Breakfast

Unfortunately many of the breakfast cereals designed specifically for children are laden with sugar. I prefer to give my children some of the more old-fashioned cereals like Weetabix, Ready Brek, Porridge or muesli and sweeten these with fresh fruit.

MAKES 1 PORTION

½ Weetabix
1 small banana

3 tablespoons mild natural yoghurt
or milk

Finely crumble the Weetabix and mash the banana. Combine all the ingredients together and serve.

Summer Fruit Muesli

Simply soak the oats overnight and stir in extra fresh fruits like peaches or strawberries the next day for a tasty nutritious muesli. If your baby is too young for lumpy food, this can be blended to a fine purée.

MAKES 4 ADULT PORTIONS

100 g / 4 oz porridge oats
2 tablespoons sultanas or raisins
300 ml / 10 fl oz freshly squeezed orange juice

2 eating apples, peeled, cored and grated
4–6 tablespoons milk
a little maple syrup or honey (for babies over 1 year)

Mix the oats, sultanas and orange juice in a bowl, cover and leave to soak overnight in the fridge. In the morning stir in the remaining ingredients and extra chopped fruit and drizzle over a little maple syrup or honey (for older children).

Mixed Cereal Muesli

As your child gets older you can let her help make up her very own muesli recipe using her favourite breakfast cereals and fruit.

MAKES 2 ADULT PORTIONS

1 tablespoon Cheerios
1 tablespoon Bran Flakes
1 Weetabix, crushed
4 slices canned peaches, cut into chunks

½ tablespoon raisins
½ small apple, peeled, cored and cut into chunks
1 dessertspoon wheatgerm

Mix all the ingredients together, varying the combination of cereals and fruits to your taste and serve with milk.

The Three Bears' Breakfast

This makes a very nutritious breakfast, but make sure your child gobbles
it up before Goldilocks comes to the front door!

MAKES 2 ADULT PORTIONS

300 ml / 10 fl oz milk
40 g / 1½ oz porridge oats

25 g / 1 oz ready-to-eat dried peaches or
apricots, chopped
1 teaspoon chopped raisins

Pour the milk into a saucepan and bring to the boil. Mix in the oats and
bring back to the boil, stirring. Add the chopped dried fruit, lower the
heat and simmer for about 4 minutes or until thickened.

Matzo Brei

For those of you who have never heard of matzo, it is a large square of
unleavened bread similar to crispbread. When uncooked, it is very brittle
and Nicholas loved to snap it into pieces and strew it all over the floor.
This is why I prefer to serve it cooked!

MAKES 2 ADULT PORTIONS

2 matzos
1 egg, beaten

25 g / 1 oz butter
a pinch of sugar (optional)

Break the matzos into bite-sized pieces and soak for a couple of minutes
in cold water. Squeeze out the excess water, then add the matzos to the
beaten egg. Melt the butter in a frying pan until sizzling and fry the matzos on both sides. Sprinkle with sugar if wished.

French Toast Cut-Outs

It's fun sometimes to cut the bread into a variety of animal shapes using biscuit cutters. For a treat, serve with maple syrup or jam.

MAKES 2 PORTIONS

1 egg
2 tablespoons milk
a pinch of cinnamon (optional)

2 slices white or raisin bread
25 g/1 oz butter

Beat the egg lightly with the milk and cinnamon, if using, and pour into a shallow dish. Dip the bread in this mixture, coating each side. Melt the butter and fry the slices or animal shapes until golden on both sides.

Cheese Scramble

Until your child is one year, scrambled egg should be cooked until it is quite firm and not runny. You could use cottage cheese instead of Cheddar.

MAKES 1 PORTION

1 egg
1 tablespoon milk
15 g/½ oz butter

1 tablespoon Cheddar cheese, finely grated
1 tomato, skinned and seeded

Beat the egg with the milk. Melt the butter over a low heat, then add the egg mixture. Cook slowly, stirring all the time. When the mixture has thickened and looks soft and creamily set, add the cheese and chopped tomato. Serve immediately.

FRUIT

Baked Apples with Raisins

Cooking apples have a better flavour, but eating apples are sweeter. You can use either for this recipe. The apples are delicious served with ice cream or custard.

MAKES 6 BABY OR 2 ADULT PORTIONS

2 apples
120 ml / 4 fl oz apple juice or water
2 tablespoons raisins
a little powdered cinnamon

1 tablespoon honey or maple syrup (if using cooking apples)
a little butter or margarine

Core the apples and prick the skins with a fork to stop them bursting. Put the apples in an ovenproof dish and pour the apple juice or water around the base. Put 1 tablespoon of the raisins into the centre of each apple, sprinkle with cinnamon and (if using cooking apples) pour over honey or maple syrup. Top each with a little butter. Bake in an oven pre-heated to 180°C (350°F) Gas 4 for about 45 minutes.

For young babies, scoop out the pulp of the apple and purée roughly with the raisins and some of the juices from the dish.

Apple and Blackberry

Blackberries and apples make a delicious combination, and the blackberries (which are rich in Vitamin C) turn the apples dark red. This also makes a super filling for a crumble (see page 167).

MAKES 6 PORTIONS

2 cooking apples, peeled, cored and chopped

100 g / 4 oz blackberries
50 g / 2 oz soft brown sugar

Cook the apples and blackberries in a saucepan with the sugar and 2 tablespoons water. Cook until the apples are soft (15–20 minutes). Put the fruit through a mouli to make into a smooth purée.

Rice Pudding with Peaches

MAKES 6 PORTIONS

50 g / 2 oz pudding rice
1 tablespoon each vanilla and caster sugars, or 2 tablespoons caster sugar
600 ml / 1 pint milk
a knob of butter

100 ml / 3½ fl oz peach juice
1 heaped tablespoon raisins
2 ripe peaches, skinned, stoned and cut into pieces

Use a little butter to grease a fairly shallow ovenproof dish. Put the rice, sugar and milk in the dish and stir well. Dot with a little butter. Bake in an oven preheated to 150°C/300°F/Gas 2 for 1½–2 hours, stirring occasionally.

Meanwhile, simmer the raisins in the peach juice and purée the peaches. When the rice pudding is cooked, stir in the peach juice, raisins and peach purée.

Fresh Pear with Semolina

This recipe is also good with apricots or apple purée with cinnamon. If you do not have any semolina, you can add a finely crushed rusk to the milk (which does not need to be boiled).

MAKES 2 PORTIONS

1 tablespoon semolina
120 ml / 4 fl oz milk
1 ripe pear, peeled, cored and sliced

2 teaspoons maple syrup
a pinch of cinnamon

Put the semolina and milk in a saucepan, bring to the boil and simmer for 2 minutes. Add the pear, maple syrup and cinnamon, then put all the ingredients through a mouli to make a purée or chop the pear finely.

Strawberry Rice Pudding

The secret of a good rice pudding is long, slow, gentle cooking. Make it after breakfast and it will be ready in time for lunch.

MAKES 6 BABY OR 3 ADULT PORTIONS

50 g / 2 oz pudding rice
½ teaspoon vanilla essence
1½ tablespoons caster sugar
600 ml / 1 pint milk

a knob of butter
strawberry jam (or blackcurrant jelly), to taste

Put the rice, vanilla essence and milk in a shallow buttered ovenproof dish and dot with a little butter. Bake in an oven preheated to 150°C (300°F) Gas 2 for 1½–2 hours, stirring occasionally. Serve hot with strawberry jam (or blackcurrant jelly) swirled into the rice pudding.

Cheese and Raisin Delight

This makes a delicious combination and is very nutritious.

MAKES 1 PORTION

25 g / 1 oz Gruyère cheese
½ apple, peeled and cored

15 g / ½ oz raisins, chopped
1 tablespoon mild natural yoghurt

Grate the Gruyère cheese and apple and mix in the raisins and yoghurt. For young babies who do not chew, put all the ingredients in a blender for about 1 minute.

☺ ☹

Dried Apricots with Papaya and Pear

Dried apricots are rich in betacarotene and iron and they combine well with a variety of fresh fruits. This is also good mixed with yoghurt. I found that my children also liked chewing on semi-dried apple rings which are easy to hold because of the hole in the middle.

MAKES 4 PORTIONS

50 g / 2 oz ready-to-eat dried apricots
½ ripe papaya, peeled, seeded and chopped

1 ripe juicy pear, peeled, cored and chopped

Put the apricots into a small saucepan and just cover with water. Bring to the boil and simmer until softened (about 8 minutes). Chop the apricots and mix with the chopped papaya and pear, or purée for babies who prefer a smoother texture.

☺ ☹ ❄

VEGETABLES
Oscar's Delight

So called because it is the same green colour as Oscar, the character from *Sesame Street*. If my son believes this is Oscar's favourite food he is much more likely to eat it himself. The egg yolk is a good source of iron.

MAKES 3 PORTIONS

75 g / 3 oz each broccoli and cauliflower, broken into small florets

1 medium courgette, sliced
1 hard-boiled egg yolk, sieved

Steam the vegetables until tender (7–8 minutes), roughly chop them and sprinkle with the sieved egg yolk, or purée together for young babies.

Cherub's Couscous

Couscous is an excellent food for babies and is very easy to prepare.

MAKES 3 PORTIONS

75 g / 3 oz sweet potato, peeled and diced
350 ml / 12 fl oz vegetable stock (see page 33)

75 g / 3 oz couscous
1 tablespoon chopped raisins (optional)
40 g / 1½ oz frozen peas

Bring the sweet potato to the boil in half the stock. Cover and simmer for 15–20 minutes. Mix the couscous and raisins in a bowl; bring the remaining stock to the boil and pour over the couscous. Cover and leave for 5 minutes. When the sweet potato is tender, add the peas and cook for a further 5 minutes. Mix the vegetables, cooking liquid and couscous, and fluff with a fork.

Lentil and Vegetable Purée

This makes a delicious purée which my nine-month-old daughter Lara loved. Lentils are an excellent source of protein and very easy to cook.

MAKES 8 PORTIONS

25 g/1 oz butter
100 g/4 oz leek, washed and sliced
175 g/6 oz carrots, peeled and chopped
50 g/2 oz split red lentils

350 ml/12 fl oz vegetable stock (see page 33) or water
100 g/4 oz cauliflower, broken into florets
½ apple, peeled, cored and chopped

Melt the butter in a saucepan and sauté the leek for about 5 minutes. Add the carrots and continue to cook for 2–3 minutes. Add the lentils, pour over the stock, bring to the boil, then cover and simmer for 10 minutes. Add the cauliflower and apple and continue to cook for about 15 minutes or until the lentils and vegetables are tender. Process in a blender to the desired consistency.

☺ ☹ ❄

Multicoloured Casserole

Babies love the bright colours and miniature size of these vegetables. It makes eating fun, and is a good lesson in finger control.

MAKES 4 PORTIONS

1 tablespoon olive oil
1 shallot, peeled and finely chopped
40 g/1½ oz red pepper, diced

100 g/4 oz frozen peas
100 g/4 oz frozen sweetcorn
120 ml/4 fl oz vegetable stock or water

eat the oil in a pan, add the shallot and red pepper and cook for 3 minutes. Add the peas and sweetcorn, pour over the vegetable stock and bring to the boil. Cover and simmer for 3–4 minutes.

☺ ☹ ❄

Cabbage Surprise

This is a delicious recipe and very simple to prepare. It makes a great lunch-time meal for the whole family; just increase the quantities, sprinkle with extra grated cheese, either Cheddar or Parmesan and brown under the grill before serving. Alternatively, after you have mixed all the ingredients together, bake in the oven at 180°C (350°F) Gas 4 for 15 minutes.

MAKES 6 PORTIONS

25 g/1 oz brown rice
75 g/3 oz cabbage, shredded
1 tomato, skinned, seeded and chopped

a little margarine or oil
50 g/2 oz Cheddar cheese, grated

ook the rice in water until quite soft (about 25 minutes). Steam the cabbage or boil in water until tender. Sauté the tomato in a little margarine or oil, add the well-drained cabbage and continue to cook for a further 2 minutes. Stir in the grated cheese and cook over a low heat until all the cheese has melted. Mix the cabbage, tomato and cheese together with the cooked rice and chop it into small pieces.

☺ ☹ ❄

Vegetables in Cheese Sauce

MAKES 6 PORTIONS

*100 g/4 oz cauliflower, broken into
florets
1 carrot, peeled and thinly sliced
50 g/2 oz frozen peas
100 g/4 oz courgettes, sliced*

Cheese Sauce
*25 g/1 oz margarine
2 tablespoons plain flour
250 ml/8 fl oz milk
50 g/2 oz Cheddar cheese, grated*

Steam the cauliflower and carrot for 6 minutes, then add the peas and courgettes and cook for a further 4 minutes. For a young baby, cook the vegetables until they are soft.

Meanwhile make the cheese sauce in the usual way (see page 59). Mash, chop or purée the vegetables with the sauce.

Green Fingers

French beans make good finger food and they are especially good with this tasty tomato sauce. Alternatively, chop the beans into short lengths and mix with the sauce.

MAKES 5 PORTIONS

*1 small onion, peeled and finely chopped
15 g/½ oz butter
175 g/6 oz French beans, trimmed*

*2 medium tomatoes, skinned
½ tablespoon tomato paste
25 g/1 oz Gruyère cheese, grated*

Sauté the onion in the butter for about 4 minutes until soft but not golden. Meanwhile steam the beans for 6–8 minutes until tender. Seed and chop the tomatoes, and mix them with the onions, tomato paste and cheese. Pour the sauce over the beans, and chop coarsely if necessary.

FISH
A Parcel of Plaice

Easy to make and all the flavour is sealed in a parcel.

MAKES 3 PORTIONS

*1 fillet (about 100 g/4 oz) plaice,
skinned*
15 g/½ oz butter, melted
*1 medium tomato, skinned, seeded and
chopped*

1 small courgette, trimmed and diced
1 dessertspoon chopped chives
1 sprig of parsley
a squeeze of lemon juice

Place the fish fillet on a piece of greased aluminium foil. Mix all the remaining ingredients together and place on top of the fish. Wrap up securely. Cook in the oven preheated to 180°C (350°F) Gas 4 for about 12 minutes or until the fish just flakes with a fork. Remove the herb sprig and mash with a fork.

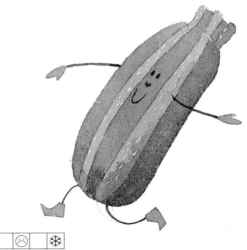

☺ ☹ ❄

Fingers of Sole

These fingers of sole are fun for babies and toddlers to eat, and make great finger food. They can be served plain or you can dip them into a home-made tomato sauce. Simply purée 3 skinned and seeded tomatoes with a sautéed shallot, 1 tablespoon tomato purée, 1 dessertspoon of milk and a teaspoon of finely chopped basil.

These 'fish fingers' are much better for your child than commercial ones, which are full of colouring and additives. If you are not using all the fingers at once, it is best to freeze them before they are cooked. You can then take out as many fingers as you need for a freshly cooked meal. Crushed cornflakes also make a delicious coating for other types of fish like haddock or cod.

MAKES 8 PORTIONS

1 shallot, peeled and finely chopped
1 dessertspoon lemon juice
1 tablespoon vegetable oil
1 sole, filleted and skinned
1 egg

1 dessertspoon milk
plain flour
crushed cornflakes
a little butter or margarine for frying

Mix together the chopped shallot, lemon juice and oil. Marinate the fish fillets in this mixture for 1 hour. Remove the fillets from the marinade. Cut them into four or five diagonal strips, depending on the size of the sole. Beat the egg together with the milk. Dip the strips first into the flour, then the egg and milk and finally the crushed cornflakes. Fry the fingers in butter until golden brown on both sides. They should take no more than a few minutes to cook.

Fillets of Sole with Grapes

Fillets of sole with grapes makes a delicious combination. This recipe is quick and easy to prepare and one that the whole family can enjoy.

MAKES 4 ADULT PORTIONS

8 single sole fillets
1 tablespoon seasoned flour
20 g/¾ oz butter
75 g/3 oz button mushrooms, thinly sliced
100 ml/3½ fl oz fish stock

100 ml/3½ fl oz double cream
1 teaspoon lemon juice
2 teaspoons chopped fresh parsley
20 seedless white grapes, halved
salt and pepper

Coat the fish with seasoned flour, melt half the butter in a large frying pan and fry the fish over a medium heat for about 2 minutes on each side until lightly golden. Transfer to a plate and keep warm.

Add the remaining butter to the pan and cook the mushrooms for 3 minutes. Add the stock and simmer for 2 minutes. Stir in the cream and lemon juice and then simmer for 2 minutes. Add the parsley and grapes, then season with salt and pepper and pour over the fish.

Haddock with Vegetables in a Cheese Sauce

Babies love bright colours, and the yellow of the sweetcorn with the red and green of the tomato and leek makes this dish look attractive. Be careful not to overcook the fish or it will become dry. Once cooked, the fish will just flake with a fork and, mixed with the cheese sauce, will be nice and soft for your baby to eat.

MAKES 6 PORTIONS

175 g/6 oz fillet of haddock, skinned
a little butter
a squeeze of lemon
25 g/1 oz leek, washed and shredded
50 g/2 oz frozen sweetcorn
1 tomato, skinned, seeded and chopped

Cheese Sauce
15 g/½ oz butter
1 tablespoon plain flour
175 ml/6 fl oz milk
40 g/1½ oz Cheddar cheese, grated

Put the fish into a suitable dish, dot with butter and add a squeeze of lemon juice. Cover with a lid and microwave for 4 minutes on High. Alternatively, cook the fish in an oven preheated to 180°C (350°F) Gas 4 for 8–10 minutes.

Sauté the leek in a knob of butter for 2 minutes. Steam the sweetcorn or cook in boiling water until tender (about 6 minutes). Make the cheese sauce in the usual way (see page 59). Flake the fish with a fork and stir it, the vegetables and tomato into the cheese sauce.

Salmon with a Creamy Chive Sauce

Salmon is easy to cook. It can be cooked very quickly in the microwave but here I have wrapped it in aluminium foil with some vegetables and herbs and cooked it more slowly to bring out the flavour.

MAKES 5 PORTIONS

100 g/4 oz fillet of salmon or 1 small
salmon cutlet
1 dessertspoon lemon juice
½ small onion, peeled and sliced
½ bay leaf
1 small tomato, cut into chunks
1 sprig of parsley
a little butter

Chive Sauce
15 g/½ oz butter
1 tablespoon plain flour
150 ml/5 fl oz milk
cooking liquid from the fish
1 dessertspoon snipped chives

Wrap the salmon in aluminium foil with the rest of the ingredients and bake in an oven preheated to 180°C (350°F) Gas 4 for 15 minutes. Meanwhile, make a white sauce, using the butter, flour and milk in the usual way (see page 59).

Once the salmon is cooked, remove it from the foil, strain off the cooking liquid and add this to the white sauce. Finally, stir the chopped chives into the sauce. Flake the salmon and pour the chive sauce over it.

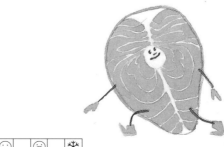

CHICKEN
Chicken with Couscous

MAKES 4 PORTIONS

15 g/½ oz butter
25 g/1 oz chopped onion
25 g/1 oz frozen peas (cooked)

175 ml/6 fl oz chicken stock
65 g/2 ½ oz quick-cooking couscous
50 g/2 oz diced cooked chicken

Melt the butter in a pan and sauté the onion until softened but not coloured. Stir in the frozen peas, pour over the stock, bring to the boil and cook for 3 minutes. Stir in the couscous, remove from the heat, cover and set aside for 6 minutes. Fluff the couscous with a fork and mix in the diced chicken.

Chicken and Apple Balls

This is a tasty recipe, very easy to make and the apple blends really well with the chicken to bring out the flavour and keep it moist. These little balls make great finger food.

MAKES 10 GOLF-BALL-SIZED PORTIONS

3 chicken breasts or 6 chicken thighs, off
the bone and skinned
1 large eating apple, peeled
1 tablespoon lemon juice
1 tablespoon chopped sage or parsley, or
a pinch of mixed dried herbs

½ small onion, peeled and finely chopped
1 crumbled chicken stock cube (for
babies over 1 year)
2 tablespoons fresh breadcrumbs
plain flour
vegetable oil

Chop the chicken very finely in a food processor and grate the apple. Mix the lemon juice with the apple. Combine chicken, apple, fresh or dried herbs, onion, finely crumbled stock cube (if using) and breadcrumbs. Form into little balls and roll in flour. Heat the oil in a frying pan and, when it is really hot, shallow-fry the balls until they are golden and cooked through (about 6 minutes).

Bang Bang Chicken

So called because my son likes to help when I flatten the chicken by banging it with a mallet! You can prepare these chicken fingers in advance. Before frying, wrap each strip separately and freeze. Just take one or two strips out of the freezer and fry them for freshly cooked chicken fingers.

MAKES 8 PORTIONS

2 chicken breasts, off the bone and skinned
3 slices wholemeal bread
1 tablespoon grated Parmesan cheese (optional)

1 tablespoon chopped parsley (optional)
2 tablespoons plain flour
1 egg, beaten
vegetable oil

Cover the chicken with greaseproof paper and flatten with a mallet or rolling pin, then cut each breast lengthways into four strips. Make breadcrumbs from the slices of bread in a food processor. If you are using the Parmesan and parsley, mix these together with the breadcrumbs in a bowl.

Dip the chicken into the flour, then into the egg and then finally into the breadcrumbs. Fry in oil for 3–4 minutes each side until golden on the outside and cooked through. Drain on absorbent kitchen paper and serve.

Chicken with Potato and Swede

A good way to gradually introduce texture is to combine chopped food with creamy mashed potatoes – this can work well with chicken, meat or fish. You could use carrot instead of swede.

MAKES 5 PORTIONS

200 g/7 oz potato, peeled and chopped
260 g/7 oz swede, peeled and chopped
75 g/3 oz chicken, cut into chunks

250 ml/8 fl oz chicken stock
20 g/¾ oz butter
3 tablespoons milk

Put the potato and swede in a saucepan, pour over some boiling water, then cover and cook over a medium heat for 20 minutes or until the vegetables are tender. Meanwhile, poach the chicken in the stock for 6–8 minutes or until cooked through (allow to cool in the stock).

Drain the swede and potato and mash together with the butter and milk. Chop the chicken into small pieces and mix with the mashed vegetables.

Chicken with Cornflakes

Cornflakes are very versatile and I often use them instead of breadcrumbs to coat both chicken and fish. These strips of chicken make good finger food. Before cooking, they can be individually wrapped and frozen.

MAKES 3–4 PORTIONS

1 egg
1 tablespoon milk
25 g/1 oz cornflakes, crushed

1 large chicken breast, skinned, off the bone and cut into about 8 strips
15 g/½ oz butter, melted

Mix together the beaten egg and milk in a shallow dish. In a separate dish spread out the cornflake crumbs. Dip the strips of chicken first into the egg and then coat with the cornflakes. Put the chicken strips into a greased ovenproof dish, drizzle over the melted butter and toss to coat. Bake in an oven preheated to 180°C (350°F) Gas 4 for about 30 minutes or until the chicken is cooked through. Alternatively, the chicken strips can be sautéed in vegetable oil until golden and cooked through.

Chicken with Summer Vegetables

In the summer, you can often find different varieties of squash – some are round, some green and some yellow. They are all delicious, but this recipe can also be made simply with courgettes.

MAKES 6 PORTIONS

1 shallot, peeled and finely chopped
¼ red sweet pepper, seeded and finely chopped
2 tablespoons vegetable oil
1 chicken breast, cut into chunks
2 tablespoons apple juice

120 ml / 4 fl oz chicken stock (see page 62)
2 medium courgettes, finely chopped, or 225 g / 8 oz summer squash, chopped
1 tablespoon chopped basil

Sauté the shallot and sweet pepper in the vegetable oil until softened. Stir in the chicken and continue to cook for about 4 minutes. Pour over the apple juice and stock and stir in the courgettes or squash and basil. Bring to the boil, then cover and simmer for about 12 minutes or until the chicken is thoroughly cooked and the vegetables are tender. Chop or purée to desired consistency.

Chicken with Winter Vegetables

This is quick and easy to prepare and has a delicious rich chicken flavour.
It is good with mashed potato.

MAKES 6 PORTIONS

2 chicken breasts, on the bone and skinned
a little flour
vegetable oil
*1 leek, white part only, washed and
sliced*

1 small onion, peeled and finely chopped
1 carrot, peeled and sliced
1 celery stalk, trimmed and sliced
*300 ml/10 fl oz chicken stock (see
page 62)*

Cut the chicken breasts in half, roll them in flour and brown them in a little oil for 3–4 minutes. In another frying pan, sauté the leek and onion in a little oil for 5 minutes until soft and golden. Put the chicken into a casserole together with all the vegetables and the stock. Cook in an oven preheated to 180°C (350°F) Gas 4 for 1 hour, stirring halfway through.

Take the chicken off the bone and chop it into little pieces with the vegetables or purée it together with the cooking liquid in a mouli or blender.

RED MEATS
Beef Casserole with Carrots

The secret for a delicious rich taste is to cook the meat for a long time so that it is very tender and has a good flavour from the onions and carrots. Increase the Marmite for toddlers.

MAKES 10 PORTIONS

2 medium onions, peeled and sliced
vegetable oil
350 g / 12 oz lean stewing beef, trimmed and cut into small chunks
2 medium carrots, peeled and sliced

1 beef stock cube, crumbled or 1 teaspoon Marmite (for babies over 1 year)
1 tablespoon chopped parsley
600 ml / 1 pint water
2 large potatoes, cut into quarters

Fry the onion until golden in a little oil, then add the meat chunks and brown. Transfer the meat and onions to a small casserole and add all the rest of the ingredients except for the potatoes. Cook, covered, in an oven preheated to 180°C (350°F) Gas 4 for 30 minutes, then turn down the heat and cook for a further 2½ hours at 160°C (325°F) Gas 3. One hour before you finish cooking the meat, add the potatoes.

Chop the meat quite finely in a food processor or blender so that it is easy for your baby to chew. If the meat gets too dry whilst cooking, add a little extra water. You can also add mushrooms and tomatoes to this recipe for variation and they should be added half an hour before the end of cooking time.

☺ ☹ ❄

Liver Casserole

I have found that mothers who do not like liver themselves seldom cook it for their children. But liver is very good for children: it is easy to digest, a good source of iron and is also very easy to cook. I must admit that I dislike the taste of liver having been forced to eat it as a child at school, but, to my great surprise, my one-year-old son adored it. This recipe is good served with mashed potato.

MAKES 8 PORTIONS

1 small onion, peeled and chopped
vegetable oil
1 large or 2 small carrots, peeled and chopped
1 tablespoon vegetable stock (see page 33)

225 g/8 oz calf's liver, trimmed and sliced
2 large tomatoes, skinned, seeded and chopped
1 dessertspoon chopped parsley

Fry the onion in a little oil until transparent. Add the chopped carrot and continue to fry for about 4 minutes. Add the stock, liver, tomatoes and parsley. Simmer over a low heat for 15–20 minutes. Cut the liver into small pieces or blend for a few seconds to make a rough purée.

Savoury Veal Casserole

A delicious casserole of veal, vegetables and fresh herbs – just increase the quantities for a meal the whole family can enjoy.

MAKES 3 PORTIONS

1 small onion, peeled and finely chopped
1 carrot, scraped and sliced
½ stick celery, sliced
vegetable oil

100 g/4 oz lean veal for stewing
1 sprig of rosemary
1 sprig of parsley
120 ml/4 fl oz water

Fry the onion, carrot and celery in a little oil for 3 minutes. Cut the veal into chunks and put it into a saucepan with the vegetables, herbs and the water. Simmer slowly, covered for 1 hour (stirring once). Remove the herbs and roughly chop the veal and vegetables in a food processor.

Special Steak

This recipe makes a very good introduction to red meat for your baby.

MAKES 4 PORTIONS

1 potato (about 225 g/8 oz), peeled and chopped
1 shallot or 25 g/1 oz onion, peeled and finely chopped
1 tablespoon vegetable oil
100 g/4 oz fillet steak

50 g/2 oz button mushrooms, washed and chopped
15 g/½ oz butter
1 tomato, skinned, seeded and chopped
2 tablespoons milk

Boil the potato until tender, then drain. Meanwhile, sauté the shallot in the vegetable oil until softened. Spoon half the shallots on to a piece of aluminium foil. Cut the steak into slices 1 cm/½ inch thick and place on top of the shallots. Spread the remaining shallots over the steak. Cook under a preheated grill for 3 minutes each side or until cooked. Sauté the button mushrooms in half the butter for 2 minutes, add the chopped tomato and continue to cook for 1 minute. Mash the potato with the milk and the remaining butter until smooth. Chop or purée the steak together with the shallots, mushrooms and tomato and mix with the mashed potato.

Mini Shepherd's Pie

Shepherd's pie was always a great 'comfort food' on a winter's evening when I was a child. Try this tasty recipe for your baby (and see page 155 for a more grown-up version).

MAKES 4 PORTIONS

¼ onion, peeled and finely chopped
1 small garlic clove, peeled and finely chopped (optional)
¼ red or green sweet pepper, seeded and finely chopped
½ tablespoon olive oil
100 g/4 oz lean minced beef
½ tablespoon chopped parsley

2 tomatoes, skinned, seeded and chopped
1 teaspoon tomato purée
120 ml/4 fl oz chicken stock
175 g/6 oz potatoes, peeled and cut into chunks
2 tablespoons milk
a generous knob of butter

Sauté the onion, garlic and diced pepper in the oil for 5 minutes until softened. Add the minced beef and parsley and cook, stirring, until browned. Add the tomatoes, tomato purée and chicken stock, bring to the boil, then cover and simmer for about 12 minutes. Meanwhile, cook the potatoes in boiling salted water, then drain and mash together with the milk and butter. Mix the mashed potato with the meat.

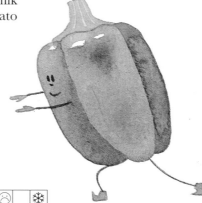

Tasty Rice with Meat and Vegetables

MAKES 8 PORTIONS

½ onion, peeled and finely chopped
1 carrot, scrubbed and finely chopped
1 tablespoon vegetable oil
225 g/8 oz lean minced beef
400 g/14 oz canned chopped tomatoes
a few drops of Worcestershire sauce

Rice
50 g/2 oz basmati rice
300 ml/10 fl oz chicken stock (see page 62)
½ small red sweet pepper, seeded and finely chopped
50 g/2 oz frozen peas

Rinse the rice and place in a saucepan with the chicken stock. Bring to the boil, then cover and simmer for 10 minutes. Add the red pepper and peas and cook, uncovered, for 6–7 minutes, or until the rice is tender and there is no liquid left.

Meanwhile sauté the onion and carrot in the vegetable oil for 5 minutes. Add the minced meat and cook, stirring, until browned. Transfer the meat into a food processor and chop for 30 seconds to make it easier for your baby to chew. Return the meat to the pan and add the tomatoes and Worcestershire sauce. Cook over a gentle heat for 10 minutes. Stir in the rice and cook for 3–4 minutes.

PASTA
Salmon and Broccoli Tagliatelle

Pasta is popular with babies and toddlers so combining it with nutritious foods like salmon and broccoli is a good idea.

MAKES 6 PORTIONS

175 g/6 oz tagliatelle
75 g/3 oz broccoli, cut into small florets
300 ml/10 fl oz milk
1 bay leaf
3 peppercorns

a sprig of parsley
150 g/5 oz fillet of salmon, skinned
15 g/½ oz butter
15 g/½ oz flour
½ teaspoon lemon juice
50 g/2 oz grated Cheddar cheese

Cook the tagliatelle according to the packet instructions. Steam the broccoli or cook in boiling water for about 4 minutes or until tender.

Pour the milk into a saucepan together with the bay leaf, peppercorns and parsley and bring to the boil. Reduce the heat, place the salmon in the pan and simmer covered for 6–8 minutes or until the fish is just cooked. Remove the salmon with a slotted spoon and strain the milk.

Melt the butter, stir in the flour and cook for 1 minute. Gradually whisk in the reserved milk. Bring to the boil and then simmer for 2 minutes. Stir in the lemon juice and cheese until melted.

Flake the fish and stir into the cheese sauce together with the broccoli cut into small pieces. Chop the tagliatelle into short lengths and mix with the cheese sauce.

☺ ☹ ❄

Bolognese Sauce with Aubergine

MAKES 12 PORTIONS OF SAUCE

1 aubergine, peeled and sliced
a little salt
1 medium onion, peeled and chopped
¼ garlic clove, peeled and chopped
vegetable oil for frying
450 g/1 lb lean minced beef or lamb

2 tablespoons tomato purée
4 tomatoes, skinned, seeded and chopped
¼ teaspoon mixed herbs
2 tablespoons plain flour
450 ml/15 fl oz chicken stock (see page 62)
100 g/4 oz mushrooms, washed and sliced

Sprinkle the aubergine with salt and drain for 30 minutes. Rinse and pat dry. Sauté the onion and garlic in oil until soft. Add the meat and cook until browned. Chop in a food processor. Return to the pan, add the tomato purée, tomatoes, herbs, flour and stock. Bring to the boil and simmer for 45 minutes. Fry the aubergine in oil until golden. Pat dry with kitchen paper. Chop in a food processor. Sauté the mushrooms in oil and add to the sauce with the aubergine.

Creamy Chicken Pasta Sauce

MAKES 3 PORTIONS OF SAUCE

1 small chicken breast, off the bone,
skinned and cut into chunks
a little oil or chicken stock, for cooking
40 g/1½ oz broccoli, broken into florets

15 g/½ oz butter
1 tablespoon flour
175 ml/6 fl oz milk
25 g/1 oz Cheddar cheese, grated

Sauté the chicken or poach in stock until cooked. Steam the broccoli until tender. Melt the butter and stir in the flour. Gradually stir in the milk over a gentle heat until thickened. Simmer for 1 minute, stirring. Off the heat, stir in the cheese. Mix in the chicken and broccoli, chop or purée and mix with cooked pasta.

Tomato and Cheese Pasta Sauce

Delicious poured over pasta and steamed vegetables. Serve 25 g/1 oz cooked pasta and 50 g/2 oz vegetables per portion.

MAKES 3 PORTIONS OF SAUCE

25 g/1 oz onion, peeled and finely chopped
1 tablespoon olive oil
4 medium tomatoes, skinned, seeded and chopped

2 tablespoons Philadelphia cream cheese
50 ml/2 fl oz milk
25 g/1 oz Cheddar cheese, grated

Sauté the onion in the olive oil until softened, then add the tomatoes and continue to cook for 3 minutes. Mix in the cream cheese and milk, then remove from the heat and stir in the grated cheese until melted. Purée in a blender to make a smooth sauce. Pour the sauce over the pasta or vegetables, which can be chopped to the desired consistency.

Mushroom, Courgette and Tomato Pasta Sauce

Choose pasta shapes that are easy for your baby to pick up with her fingers. This creamy sauce will stick to the pasta. If your baby prefers to be spoon-fed, choose very small pasta shapes or chop them into pieces.

MAKES 4 PORTIONS OF SAUCE

25 g/1 oz butter
1 tablespoon plain flour
175 ml/6 fl oz milk
100 g/4 oz button mushrooms, washed and sliced

2 courgettes, sliced
2 medium tomatoes, skinned, seeded and chopped
1 teaspoon chopped basil

To make the creamy sauce, use half the butter, with the flour and the milk, and make in the usual way (see page 59). Sauté the mushrooms in half the remaining butter for 2 minutes. Mix them together with the white sauce and purée in a blender.

Steam the courgettes until tender (about 10 minutes). Sauté the tomatoes together with the basil in the remaining butter for 1 minute.

Pour the mushroom sauce over cooked pasta and stir in the tomatoes and courgettes.

☺ ☹ ❄

Tuna Salad

Oily fish like tuna and salmon contain omega-3 fatty acids which help prevent heart disease and are also important for brain and visual development.

MAKES 4 PORTIONS

75 g/3 oz cooked pasta bows or shells
1 spring onion, finely chopped, or
1 small shallot, peeled and diced
100 g/4 oz canned tuna in oil, drained
and flaked
3 cherry tomatoes, quartered
25 g/1 oz canned sweetcorn (or cooked
frozen sweetcorn)
½ small avocado, peeled, stoned and cut
into small cubes

Dressing
1 tablespoon mayonnaise
1 tablespoon olive oil
1 teaspoon fresh lemon juice

Mix together the ingredients for the dressing. Combine the cooked pasta with the salad ingredients and toss with the dressing. If wished, toast some sesame seeds in a dry frying pan until golden and sprinkle these on top.

NINE TO TWELVE MONTH MEAL PLANNER

	Breakfast	Sleep	Lunch
Day 1	**Fruity Swiss Muesli** **Dried Apricot with Papaya and Pear** served with yoghurt Milk	Milk	**Chicken and Apple Balls** Finger vegetables **Strawberry Rice Pudding** Water
Day 2	Weetabix Cheese on toast Fruit Milk	Milk	**Special Steak** **Home-Made Fruit Jelly** Fruit Water
Day 3	Scrambled egg with toast Fruit with cottage cheese Milk	Milk	**Fillets of Fish in an Orange Sauce** **Baked Apples with Raisins** Water
Day 4	**Cheese and Raisin Delight** Cheerios (or other cereal) Fruit Milk	Milk	**Liver Casserole** **Multicoloured Casserole** Papaya purée Water
Day 5	**French Toast Cut-Outs** **Apricot, Apple and Pear Custard** Milk	Milk	**Bang Bang Chicken** **Cabbage Surprise** **Home-Made Fruit Jelly** Fruit Water
Day 6	**Summer Fruit Muesli** Yoghurt with dried fruit Milk	Milk	**Beef Casserole with Carrots** **Going Bananas** Water
Day 7	**Cheese Scramble** **Fruity Yoghurt** Milk	Milk	**Chicken with Couscous** **Fresh Pear with Semolina** Water

Mid Afternoon	Dinner	Bedtime
Milk	Finger sandwiches Finger vegetables Juice or water	Milk
Milk	**Pasta with Tomato and Cheese Pasta Sauce** Fromage frais/Yoghurt Juice or water	Milk
Milk	**Courgette and Pea Souper** Fruit Juice or water	Milk
Milk	**Vegetables in Cheese Sauce** **Apple and Blackberry** Juice or water	Milk
Milk	**Tomato and Courgette Pasta Stars** Fruit Juice or water	Milk
Milk	**Fingers of Sole** Finger vegetables **Rice Pudding with Peaches** Juice or water	Milk
Milk	**Lentil and Vegetable Purée** Sticks of cheese **Baked Apples with Raisins** Juice or water	Milk

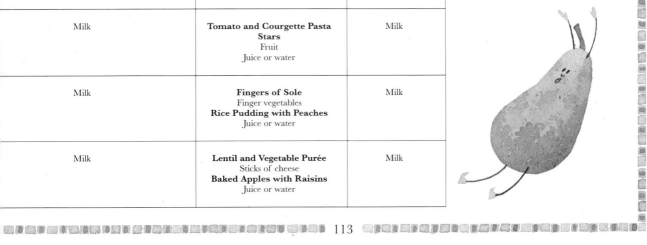

CHAPTER FIVE

TODDLERS

I find that, beyond the age of one, toddlers prefer to exercise their independence and feed themselves. The more your toddler experiments using a spoon and fork, the quicker he will master the art of feeding himself – you never know, some food might find its way into his mouth! A handy tip is to put a clean towel or a baby's plastic splash mat under his high chair to catch the food that gets dropped over the side; this will make sure the food is still clean and can be given back to your child. A 'pelican' bib – a strong plastic bib which has a tray at the bottom to catch stray food – is also good. If your toddler has difficulty eating with a spoon, try giving him finger foods like goujons of fish or raw vegetables with a dip. You must still be careful, though, to keep food like olives, nuts or fresh lychees out of the reach of young children. Toddlers love to put everything in their mouths and it would be so easy for them to choke on such foods.

ENJOYING MEALTIMES
TOGETHER

Toddlers, unlike adults, do not have strict meal times. They are probably more sensible than us and will eat when they are hungry, and no amount of coaxing will get them to eat when they are not. Many toddlers prefer lots of small meals during the day to three main meals. In fact doctors have proved that this is a healthier way of eating. There is plenty of time when he grows older and when he goes to school to establish a regular meal pattern. There is a whole section in this book on healthy snacks, so do not make the mistake of giving your toddler sweets or processed snacks when he could enjoy eating a dip with a bowl of raw vegetables much more. Toddlers who get used to eating healthy snacks are more likely to continue the same habits later on in life. However, it would also be wrong to make sweets and doughnuts the forbidden fruit, as your toddler would crave them all the more and gorge himself on them whenever he could.

Many toddlers enjoy eating much more sophisticated food than we would imagine possible. Let your child try food from your plate and you may be very surprised by the tastes he enjoys. Of course, food from Mummy's or Daddy's plate is much more interesting than his own meal and you can sometimes entice your child to eat if you put his meal on your plate. But the point at this stage is that the toddler can now eat, to a large extent, what you adults are eating. I am a great believer in giving toddlers 'grown-up' foods as soon as possible and almost all the recipes that follow are suitable for the whole family. *Do* eat with your child rather than just sit there shovelling food into his mouth. He'll eat much more happily *with* you – after all, who enjoys eating alone?

Try and reform your own eating habits by adding less salt and sugar to your food and your toddler will be able to enjoy almost everything you cook. So, I hope that you will enjoy many happy mealtimes together and that your children will introduce you to some great new recipes!

MY CHILD WON'T EAT!

After the age of one, your child will be expending much more energy and nearly all toddlers at some stage will lose interest in food and would much rather play with their toys and run around. This can be a very difficult time and it is important not to make a big fuss if your child refuses to eat. He will eat when he is hungry and, the more you fuss, the more he will refuse his food. Be patient with him – he will grow out of this phase.

If your toddler really enjoys his food and eats well at mealtimes, then you really are a lucky mother. I know so many mothers who worry constantly that their child is not eating enough. Most of these worries are unnecessary and toddlers can thrive very well on remarkably little food.

Toddlers are very unpredictable: some days they will be ravenous, and other days they will eat practically nothing. If you judge a child's food intake over a whole week, you won't worry as much if one day he refuses to eat anything.

Many mothers complain that their toddler will not touch meat or fish, but there are lots of other equally good sources of protein like peanut butter, eggs or dairy produce. Then there are the mothers who are tearing their hair out because their children will only eat one thing. This is also quite normal: children, unlike adults, like repetition in their diet and they are often wary of trying new foods. Very often, if you let your child choose his own diet, you would be surprised that he might, without any coaxing on your part, choose a balanced one.

There are several ways in which you can encourage your child to eat. You might vary the venue of his meals. My son enjoyed eating his meals in the playhouse in the garden. He also loved to have a little tea party and invite his favourite teddy bears; we laid food on a low table in his playroom, he pretended to feed the bears and then ate the food himself. It is all part of a game and he loved it. Eating becomes fun and is no longer a battle of wills.

Toddlers enjoy playing with food and they are interested in the feel of different foods. It is a good idea sometimes to let your child help prepare his meals. For example, he could help you stir the jelly or shell the peas. This is all part of a learning process, and food should be fun. Let your toddler poke his finger into the jelly and see it wobble – there is plenty of time to teach him table manners once he has finished experimenting. You may well stimulate an interest in food by getting him to 'help' (under supervision, of course). My son is always willing to lend a helping hand, especially when it comes to making biscuits. He loves to knead the dough, roll it out and cut it into shapes, and it is much more fun than play dough!

Letting toddlers experiment with different spoons and forks and praising them when they manage to get the food into their mouth is another way to encourage them to eat. We have little Chinese meals at home and I feed them with chopsticks. You should see how they enjoy it and how wide they open their mouths!

A great deal of problem eating can be overcome by attractive presentation. We can learn a lot from the Japanese, who believe that food should please the eye as well as the stomach. Colour is very important and it is interesting that most toddlers go for the brightly coloured foods first. Try to choose contrasting colours to make the food look appealing. It is a good idea to use plastic plates with separate compartments (you can buy these in most supermarkets) and present your toddler with two or three foods in separate sections – but keep the dessert out of sight until the main course has been eaten!

Sometimes it is fun to arrange food in a pattern on the plate. You can help teach your child by arranging food in the shape of numbers or letters or make the food into the shape of a face. You can use some small-sized novelty biscuit cutters to cut out shapes from bread, sandwiches or cheese to stimulate your child's interest. Another tip is to call food by funny names like Peter Rabbit carrots or Noddy soup. You may laugh, but if your toddler thinks this is what his favourite character eats for lunch, he is more likely to eat it himself!

Never put too much food on a plate – much better that he should ask for more. Toddlers love individual portions of food. Make a miniature shepherd's pie (see page 155), for example (much nicer than a dollop of meat and potatoes on a plate) and miniature cakes rather than slices from a large cake.

If you have given your toddler a good choice of foods and he still refuses to eat, it is not, then, a good idea to offer him the contents of the fridge and larder. Explain that this is his meal and that there is nothing else on offer. If he is very restless and clearly not interested, just put the food back in the fridge and bring it out a little later. You will be making a rod for your own back otherwise, and nine times out of ten he is just not hungry. Adults are conditioned into eating three meals a day but toddlers will only eat when they are hungry – and no child has ever starved to death through stubbornness.

If you make eating fun, then your children will be tucking in with you. Eat as a family as much as possible. An occasional trip to a restaurant does wonders to stimulate a child's appetite. Even just going to a friend's house for tea can help sometimes, especially if there is another child present who likes to tuck in!

THE FOODS TO CHOOSE

Now that your child is twelve months old, you can switch from formula to whole cow's milk. Do not give him skimmed milk. Children over one year need 400 ml/²⁄₃ pint of whole milk a day. For children who are really picky, there may be advantages to continuing with a follow-on formula (which is fortified with vitamins and iron) until two years of age. Unless he is really obese, he will need a diet that contains at least 40 per cent fat; and unless obesity runs in your family, the chances are that you do not need to worry about it. Growing children need more dietary fat than adults and should not be given low-fat produce. Fat is a rich source of both the fatty acids and the fat-soluble vitamins needed for a child's growth. Also fat is concentrated calories and provides almost twice as much energy as either proteins or carbohydrates. There are, of course, exceptions to this rule, and an overweight toddler should have his fat intake restricted. In general terms, stick to healthy cooking, cutting fat from meat and cooking with vegetable fats rather than animal or saturated fats.

Vegetable dishes at this stage can be served to the whole family as a main meal. This is useful if your child goes through a stage of refusing to eat any meat and you need to supplement his diet with protein-rich foods like nuts, beans, pulses and soya products. (It's also vital for children who are being brought up as vegetarians.)

You can now include healthy 'convenience' fish like canned tuna and salmon, which are cheaper than fresh fish. Chicken dishes, too, can be more versatile – I've

tried to make this a fairly international section. Chicken is so low in fat, and such a favourite with us, that I'm sure one day my husband will turn into one, the amount he eats!

Although more and more people are turning away from red meat in favour of

fish and chicken, you must bear in mind that red meat provides more iron and zinc than either fish or poultry and that you should supplement your child's diet by providing other sources of these minerals – leafy green vegetables, beans, lentils and eggs, for instance. You could offer your toddler foods like hamburgers and shepherd's pie, so long as they are lean – you can ask your butcher to mince some lean cuts especially for you. Do not give your toddler processed meats like sausages, salami or corned beef.

Pasta remained a great favourite with my toddlers. There is a wonderful variety available to choose from; you can stuff cannelloni, make a tomato sauce for fresh ravioli containing Ricotta and spinach, or entice your child to eat meat by making spaghetti bolognese. (My son, Nicholas, who shows little enthusiasm for eating minced meat, will gobble it all up if it is stuffed inside cannelloni or served as a spaghetti sauce.) You can even teach your toddler to read by buying alphabet spaghetti! Individual pieces of pasta like *penne* (tubes) or *papardelle* (bow-ties) are still much easier for toddlers to eat than long strands of spaghetti. (Although Nicholas, when twenty months, invented his own method of eating spaghetti – he held it out in front of him by the two ends and sucked in from the middle! Not the height of good manners perhaps, but certainly very efficient.)

Fruit and Desserts

There are many recipes here for cold and cooked desserts which can be enjoyed by the whole family, but there is still nothing more delicious or better for you and your child than fresh ripe fruit. None of the vitamins and nutrients are destroyed through cooking, and it makes great finger food for your toddler. My son adores fruit so much that we have had to hide the fruit bowl until he finishes his main course! He would far rather eat fruit than sickly sweet puddings and chocolates. Serve fruit on a daily basis and one of these desserts every now and again as a treat.

Present fresh fruit in an attractive way: contrast colours on the plate, cut the fruits into interesting shapes and arrange in patterns. Always make sure that you remove any stones before giving to your toddler, as he could so easily choke.

Where raw fruit is concerned, there are endless variations on a theme. Purée or grate fruits and mix them with cottage cheese or yoghurt and wheatgerm. Cut the fruit into bite-sized chunks and cover with yoghurt and honey or home-made custard. Dried fruits like apricots, peaches and apple rings make great finger foods.

Try giving your children some more exotic fruits like sharon fruit, which looks like an orange tomato and is grown in Israel. It tastes wonderful mashed with yoghurt (see page 48) and can be found in large supermarkets when it is in season. One kiwi fruit supplies more than the daily adult requirement of Vitamin C and makes a good snack cut into slices, and mango and papaya blend very well with dairy produce.

Fruits can also be puréed for use in ice creams. Ice creams in all colours, shapes and sizes are sold all over the world. However, the quality of some products has nothing to do with the true home-

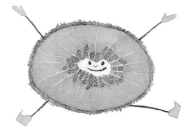

made experience. I think that there is nothing to beat the combination of milk, cream or yoghurt and wonderful home-made fruit purées – far better for all of us than ingredients like vegetable fat, glucose syrup, whey solids, guar gum, emulsifier (E471), stabilisers and artificial flavours that can be found in many commercial ice creams lingering in the deep freezes of supermarkets. In Britain alone, on average £400 million pounds a year is spent on ice cream and there *are* some good commercial brands made from natural ingredients only, but you do need to look out for them.

If you enjoy making your own ice cream it really is worth investing in a small ice-cream-making machine. Believe me, you will put it to good use through the years and your children will be very popular with their friends when they come round for tea. If you do not have an ice-cream maker, do not be put off making your own home-made ice creams. Just pour the prepared mixture into a plastic container, cover with foil or a polythene bag and place in the freezer until firm (3–4 hours). Break the mixture into pieces, put it into a food processor bowl and beat with a metal blade until light and fluffy but not thawed. This should get rid of the ice particles in the mixture and, for a really smooth texture, it is advisable to repeat this process at least twice during freezing. Put the ice cream back into the freezer in the plastic container. Ice cream tastes best

if you take it out of the freezer 10 minutes before you serve it.

Also try making your own ice-lollies using fresh fruit and fruit juice – toddlers love these (see page 169).

Baking for Toddlers

A toddler's first birthday is a big occasion in his life and probably even more exciting for his parents and grandparents! It is great fun preparing the food for a child's party. Anyone can go to a shop and order a birthday cake in the shape of a train, but how much more impressive and satisfying it is to bake and decorate your own. Your child will love to help with the mixing and decorating – probably more fun than eating it.

Any basic sponge or fruit-cake mixture could be adapted to a novelty shape, if you like. There are many smaller cakes that can be served at a child's tea party. Many of the baking recipes contain healthy ingredients, cutting out undesirables as much as possible, but some are sheer uncompromised treats.

Healthy Snacks

If your toddler is happy to eat three main meals a day, then that is wonderful and very convenient for everyone, but – let's face it – nearly all toddlers snack between meals. Whereas for some this just supplements their main meals, many toddlers do not have the patience to sit down and eat a proper meal and they get most of their nutrition from snacks during the day. Toddlers' stomachs are small and it is often difficult for them to eat enough at breakfast, say, to last them until lunchtime when they have been rushing around all morning. As I said earlier, lots of small meals – healthy snacks – during the day are in fact healthier than three main meals. Snacks are therefore a very important part of a toddler's diet. If you encourage your child when he is very young to enjoy eating healthy snacks in preference to sweets and crisps, it is likely that he will continue these habits later in life and enjoy a much healthier diet.

Keep your larder and fridge full of healthy snacks and, when you take your toddler out, try to remember to take a small bag of healthy snacks with you. Toddlers expend a lot of energy and it doesn't take them long to get hungry again after a meal.

TEXTURES AND QUANTITIES

There is no longer any need to purée your child's food; on the contrary, he should be getting used to chewing. The longer you continue with purées because that is the way your child prefers his food, the more difficult it will become to encourage him to chew and swallow his food properly. In fact chewing on something hard like a raw carrot should help to relieve sore gums. A lot of toddlers, however, do not like to chew chunks of meat, and it is sometimes necessary to break meat down in a blender before serving. I find that minced meat, liver or chicken goes down better with most toddlers than chunks of meat.

With each recipe in this chapter, I have given quantities in adult portions. Every child is different, and you must gauge the portion size on your toddler's appetite. He can eat anything from a quarter of an adult portion to a whole portion if he is exceptionally hungry and greedy! (If your toddler is becoming overweight, then you should consult your doctor and consider putting him on a low-fat diet.)

VEGETABLES
Ratatouille with Rice or Pasta

Vegetables tend to be quite soft in ratatouille and so are easy for your toddler to chew. Choose a firm aubergine and courgette; if they are not fresh, the ratatouille may taste bitter. Serve as an accompaniment to a meal with rice, as below, or with pasta shapes. It is suitable for freezing without the rice.

MAKES 4 ADULT PORTIONS

2 tablespoons olive oil
1 red onion, peeled and chopped
1 garlic clove, peeled and crushed
1 small red sweet pepper and 1 small
green sweet pepper, seeded and diced
1 courgette, trimmed and diced
1 small aubergine, trimmed and diced
400 g/14 oz canned chopped tomatoes

pinch of sugar
1 teaspoon red wine vinegar
salt and pepper

Rice
1 vegetable stock cube
1 bay leaf
200 g/7 oz long-grain rice

Heat the oil in a large saucepan and cook the onion and garlic for 1–2 minutes. Add the peppers and courgette and cook for 4–5 minutes. Add the aubergine and cook for 5 minutes. Stir in the chopped tomatoes, sugar and red wine vinegar, bring to a simmer and then cook for 10 minutes. Season with salt and pepper.

For the rice, place the vegetables, crumbled stock cube and bay leaf in a large pan of water. Stir in the rice and cook according to the packet instructions.

Special Fried Rice

Babies love rice and this is very appealing as it is so colourful. For older children you can make little sailing boats. Cut a cooked red pepper in half, stuff each half with rice and stick two corn chips upright in the rice to look like sails.

MAKES 6 ADULT PORTIONS

225 g/8 oz basmati rice
75 g/3 oz carrots, scrubbed and diced
75 g/3 oz frozen peas
75 g/3 oz green or red sweet pepper, seeded and diced

2 eggs, lightly beaten
3 tablespoons vegetable oil or vegetable oil with a teaspoon of sesame oil
1 small onion, peeled and finely chopped
1 spring onion, finely sliced
a little soy sauce (optional)

Wash the rice thoroughly and cook according to the packet instructions in a saucepan of lightly salted water until tender. Steam the carrot, peas and pepper for 5 minutes or until tender. Season the eggs with a little salt and fry them in 1 tablespoon of the oil until set, then cut into thin strips. Meanwhile, put 2 tablespoons of oil into a wok or frying pan and sauté the chopped onion until softened. Add the steamed vegetables and rice and cook, stirring, for 2–3 minutes. Add the egg and spring onion and cook, stirring, for 2 minutes more. If you like, sprinkle with a little soy sauce before serving.

Stuffed Potatoes

Stuffed potatoes make an excellent meal for toddlers and there are endless variations on the fillings you can make. Prick medium potatoes all over and brush with oil. Bake in an oven preheated to 190°C (375°F) Gas 5 for $1\frac{1}{4}$–$1\frac{1}{2}$ hours, or until tender (or you can bake them in the microwave). Carefully spoon the soft flesh out of the skins, leaving enough round the sides so that the skins keep their shape. You are now ready to make the various fillings.

Vegetable and Cheese Potato Filling

MAKES 4 ADULT PORTIONS

25 g/1 oz each broccoli and cauliflower,
broken into small florets
4 medium or 2 large baked potatoes
15 g/½ oz butter
120 ml/4 fl oz milk

50 g/2 oz Cheddar cheese, grated
2 medium tomatoes, skinned and cut
into small pieces
½ teaspoon salt
grated cheese to finish

Steam the broccoli and cauliflower until they are tender (about 6 minutes), then chop finely. Meanwhile, mash the potato flesh with the butter and milk until smooth and creamy. Mix in the cheese, tomatoes, cooked chopped vegetables and salt, and scoop the mixture back into the potato skins. Sprinkle a little extra grated cheese on top and brown under the grill.

Salmon and Sweetcorn Potato Filling

You could also add three or four sliced button mushrooms, which have been sautéed in a little butter, to the filling.

MAKES 2 ADULT PORTIONS

2 medium baked potatoes
200 g / 7 oz canned salmon, drained
75 g / 3 oz canned or cooked frozen sweetcorn
1 tablespoon chopped parsley

1 teaspoon lemon juice
75 g / 3 oz grated Cheddar cheese
salt and pepper
1 tablespoon olive oil

Cut the baked potatoes in half and scoop out the flesh, leaving the crispy skin as a shell. Mix the potato with the salmon, sweetcorn, parsley, lemon juice and Cheddar and season with salt and pepper. Spoon the filling back into the potato skins, place on a baking tray and drizzle over the olive oil. Cook for 10 minutes in an oven preheated to 180°C (350°F) Gas 4 until lightly golden on top.

Stuffed Tomatoes

Another easy dish, which can be prepared in advance and which looks
very appealing.

MAKES 2 ADULT PORTIONS

2 eggs
2 medium tomatoes
1 tablespoon mayonnaise

1 tablespoon snipped chives
salt and pepper

Hard-boil both the eggs. Meanwhile, skin the tomatoes, then cut the
tops off and scoop out the inside. Discard the seeds but keep the tiny
bits of flesh. When the eggs are ready, peel and mash them together with
the pieces of tomato, mayonnaise, chives and a little salt and pepper. Stuff
into the tomatoes and replace the tomato tops on the egg mixture.

Tasty Peanut Rissoles

Combining vegetables with nuts makes a good high-protein meal for your
toddler and this is a delicious combination that the rest of the family will
enjoy too!

MAKES 8 RISSOLES

1 onion, peeled and finely chopped
vegetable oil
1 celery stalk, diced
1 carrot, scraped and diced
½ red sweet pepper, seeded and diced
*100 g / 4 oz mushrooms, washed and
diced*

50 g / 2 oz green beans
50 g / 2 oz unsalted roasted peanuts
50 g / 2 oz cooked brown rice
½ lightly beaten egg
salt and freshly ground pepper
*100 g / 4 oz brown bread made into
breadcrumbs*

Peanuts can cause allergic reactions (see page 15).

Fry the onion in 2 tablespoons oil for 4 minutes, then add the celery, carrot and red pepper until softened. Add the mushrooms and continue to fry until soft. Drain off any excess fat.

Chop the beans and nuts in a food processor and add these to the rest of the cooked vegetables along with the rice. Stir in the beaten egg to moisten, a little seasoning and half the breadcrumbs and mix well.

Form the mixture into flat round rissoles and roll them in the remaining breadcrumbs. Put the rissoles in the fridge to harden for 1 hour. When you are ready to eat, shallow-fry the rissoles in hot oil.

Carrot and Courgette Croquettes

These are quick and easy to make. They are a good way to encourage your child to eat more vegetables and also make a tasty accompaniment to a family meal.

MAKES 6 RISSOLES

75 g/3 oz carrot, peeled
75 g/3 oz courgette, trimmed
75 g/3 oz potato, peeled
1 medium onion, peeled
3 tablespoons ground almonds

2 tablespoons plain flour
2 tablespoons lightly beaten egg
salt and pepper to taste
vegetable oil for frying

Grate the carrot, courgette, potato and onion. Cup small handfuls of the grated vegetables in the palm of your hand and squeeze out the excess moisture. Put the vegetables in a bowl and mix with the almonds, flour and egg. Season to taste. Using your hands, form into six rissoles and sauté in vegetable oil until golden on both sides and cooked through (about 6 minutes).

My Favourite Spanish Omelette

This is good served cold and cut into wedges the next day. I give
suggestions on the right for additions to the basic omelette.

MAKES 4 ADULT PORTIONS

3 tablespoons olive oil
175 g/6 oz potatoes, peeled and cut
into 1 cm/½ inch cubes
1 onion, peeled and finely chopped
½ small red sweet pepper, seeded and
chopped
50 g/2 oz frozen peas
4 eggs
2 tablespoons freshly grated Parmesan
salt and pepper

Suggested Variations
2 tablespoons Gruyère instead of
Parmesan
1 large chopped tomato
OR
50 g/2 oz mushrooms, sliced
1 tablespoon snipped chives
OR
100 g/4 oz cooked ham or bacon, cubed
50 g/2 oz sweetcorn instead of peas

Heat the oil in a non-stick 18 cm/
7 inch frying pan. Fry the potato
and onion for 5 minutes, then add the
sweet pepper and continue to cook for
5 minutes. Add the peas and cook for a further 5 minutes. Beat the eggs
together with 1 tablespoon water and the Parmesan, and season with salt
and pepper. Pour this mixture over the vegetables and cook for 5 minutes
or until the omelette is almost set. To finish, brown the top under a preheated grill for about 3 minutes or until golden. (You can wrap the handle
of the frying pan with silver foil to prevent it burning if necessary.) Cut into
wedges and serve with salad. ☺ ☹

Vegetarian Rissoles

These rissoles are delicious hot or cold and the pine nuts give them a nice crunch. They make a great meal for the whole family served with baked beans or salad. They could also be eaten in a hamburger bun with salad and ketchup.

MAKES 12–14 RISSOLES

250 g/9 oz peeled potato
200 g/7 oz peeled sweet potato
200 g/7 oz peeled parsnip
150 g/5 oz broccoli, cut into florets
1 tablespoon olive oil
1 onion, peeled and finely chopped
1 garlic clove, peeled and crushed
150 g/5 oz button mushrooms, diced

2 tablespoons pine nuts
75 g/3 oz Cheddar cheese, grated
1 tablespoon tomato ketchup
a few drops of Worcestershire sauce
salt and pepper
dried bradcrumbs for coating
2 tablespoons vegetable oil for frying

Cut the potato, sweet potato and parsnip into equal-sized chunks and cook in boiling salted water until tender. Drain and then mash. Cook the broccoli in boiling salted water for 4–6 minutes until tender. Drain and then break up lightly with a wooden spoon. Heat the olive oil in a saucepan and sauté the onion and garlic for 5 minutes until soft. Add the mushrooms and pine nuts and cook for 3–4 minutes. Stir into the mashed potatoes together with the broccoli, cheese, Worcestershire sauce and tomato ketchup and then season with salt and pepper.

Leave to cool before shaping into rissoles. Coat in dried breadcrumbs and then sauté until golden in vegetable oil.

Vegetable Salad with Raspberry Vinegar

This is a refreshing salad for a summer's lunch. The dressing complements the nutty flavour of the sweetcorn and adds a little sweetness to the salad.

MAKES 4 ADULT PORTIONS

100 g/4 oz cauliflower, broken into small florets
100 g/4 oz French beans, trimmed
175 g/6 oz frozen sweetcorn
sugar to taste
¼ small lettuce, shredded
8 cherry tomatoes, cut in half

1 hard-boiled egg, grated

Dressing
1 tablespoon raspberry vinegar
2 tablespoons hazelnut oil
salt and pepper to taste

Steam the cauliflower and beans until tender (about 15 minutes). Cook the frozen sweetcorn for about 4 minutes in boiling water with a little sugar and salt. When the cauliflower, beans and sweetcorn have cooled, put all the salad ingredients in a bowl with the grated egg sprinkled on top. Mix the dressing together with a fork and pour it over the salad.

My Favourite Pasta with Broccoli

This is very simple and quick to prepare but it is a great favourite with my three children.

MAKES 4 CHILD PORTIONS

175 g/6 oz fusilli pasta
175 g/6 oz broccoli, cut into florets
25 g/1 oz butter
½ tablespoon sunflower oil

1 onion, peeled and finely chopped
1 garlic clove, peeled and crushed
1 chicken stock cube dissolved in
120 ml/4 fl oz boiling water

Cook the pasta according to the packet instructions. Steam the broccoli for 4 minutes, then set aside. Put the butter and oil in a wok and sauté the onion and garlic for 3 minutes. Add the steamed broccoli and stir-fry for 1 minute. Stir in the chicken stock, add the cooked, drained pasta and heat through.

Mini Pizzas with Puff Pastry Base

Ready-rolled puff pastry from the supermarket makes a good base for these delicious individual pizzas. You can vary the toppings, maybe adding extras such as mushrooms, ham or pepperoni.

MAKES 4 INDIVIDUAL PIZZAS

1 tablespoon tomato purée
1 tablespoon olive oil
pinch of mixed dried herbs
salt and pepper to taste
350 g/12 oz ready-rolled puff pastry

4 spring onions, trimmed and sliced
4 tablespoons frozen sweetcorn
2 slices salami, cut into thin strips,
or peperoni (optional)
100 g/4 oz mozzarella cheese, cubed

Place the tomato purée, olive oil and dried herbs in a small saucepan. Season with salt and pepper. Bring to the boil and simmer for 5 minutes until thickened. Cut four 15 cm/6 inch circles out of the pastry (you could cut around a saucer) and place these on an oiled baking sheet. Using a sharp knife, score a circle 5 mm/¼ inch from the edge of the pastry to form a rim.

Divide the tomato mixture between the pastry bases and spread evenly. Sprinkle over the spring onions, sweetcorn and salami (if using) and top with the mozzarella cheese. Season with salt and pepper. Bake in an oven preheated to 180°C (350°F) Gas 4 for 16–18 minutes.

FISH

Grandma's Gefilte Fish

This is my mother's traditional recipe. It is very appealing to children because of the slightly sweet taste of the balls. My son, Nicholas, loves them and they are very easy for him to hold and eat himself. Adults can eat them with horseradish sauce.

MAKES ABOUT 20 BALLS

1 onion, peeled and chopped very finely
in the food processor
25 g / 1 oz butter
450 g / 1 lb minced fish fillet (mix any
of the following: haddock, bream,
whiting, cod or hake)

1 egg, beaten
2 dessertspoons sugar
salt and pepper to taste
light cooking oil for frying

Sauté the onion in the butter until lightly golden. Add to the remaining ingredients and mix well. Shape into golf-ball-sized balls. Fry carefully until golden brown all over. Drain on kitchen paper. Serve hot or cold.

Salmon Fishcakes

Salmon is a good source of omega-3 fatty acids which are important for brain and visual development. Doctors recommend including at least one oil-rich fish dish a week to keep the heart in good shape. These fishcakes taste good hot or cold.

MAKES 12 MINI FISHCAKES

300 g/11 oz potatoes, peeled and cut into chunks
15 g/½ oz butter
400 g/14 oz canned red salmon
½ small onion, peeled and diced

2 spring onions, finely chopped
2 tablespoons tomato ketchup
salt and pepper
matzo meal or flour for coating
oil for frying

Boil the potatoes in a pan of lightly salted water until tender. Drain and mash together with the butter. Drain and flake the salmon and mix with the mashed potato, finely chopped onion, spring onions and tomato ketchup. Season with salt and pepper. Form into about 12 mini fishcakes and coat in matzo meal or flour. If you have time, set these aside in the fridge to firm up. Heat the oil in a large frying pan and fry the fishcakes until golden.

Nursery Fish Pie

A good, old-fashioned favourite.

MAKES 6 ADULT PORTIONS

350 g / 12 oz fillet of cod skinned, or
175 g / 6 oz fillets of both cod and
salmon
350 ml / 12 fl oz milk
1 bay leaf
4 peppercorns
a sprig of parsley
salt and pepper
25 g / 1 oz butter
25 g / 1 oz plain flour
25 g / 1 oz grated Cheddar cheese

2 tablespoons chopped chives
½ tablespoon chopped dill (optional)
2 teaspoons lemon juice
1 hard-boiled egg, chopped

Topping
550 g / 1¼ lb potatoes, peeled and cut
into pieces
25 g / 1 oz butter plus 15 g / ½ oz butter
for dotting on top
2 tablespoons milk

Put the fish in a saucepan with the milk, bay leaf, peppercorns and parsley and season with salt and pepper. Bring to the boil and then simmer, uncovered, for 8–10 minutes. While the fish is cooking, cook the potatoes for the topping in boiling lightly salted water until soft. Drain well, then mash together with 25 g / 1 oz of the butter and the milk.

Drain the fish, reserving the cooking liquid. Melt the butter in a heavy-bottomed saucepan and stir in the flour. Cook gently for 1 minute, then whisk in the fish liquid gradually and bring to the boil. Simmer the sauce for 2–3 minutes, stirring continuously until smooth. Take off the heat, and stir in the grated cheese until melted. Flake the fish and fold in together with the chives, dill (if using), lemon juice and boiled egg . Season to taste. Place the fish in an ovenproof dish (a 15 cm / 6 inch diameter and 4.5 cm / 3 inch deep round dish is perfect) and top with the mashed potato. Bake in the oven preheated to 180°C (350°F) Gas 4 for 15–20 minutes. Dot with the remaining butter and grill for about 2 minutes until brown and crispy.

Fish in Creamy Mushroom Sauce

For older children, cook 225 g/8 oz fresh spinach and lay each whole
fillet on a bed of spinach and pour over the sauce.

MAKES 4 ADULT PORTIONS

1 small onion, peeled and finely chopped
40 g/1½ oz butter
225 g/8 oz button mushrooms, washed
and finely chopped
2 tablespoons lemon juice

2 tablespoons chopped parsley
2 tablespoons plain flour
300 ml/10 fl oz milk
1 sole or plaice, filleted

Fry the onion in half the butter until transparent. Add the mushrooms,
lemon juice and parsley and cook for 2 minutes. Add the flour and
cook for 2 minutes, stirring constantly. Add the milk gradually and cook,
stirring constantly, until the sauce is thick and smooth.

Fry the sole fillets in the rest of the butter for 2–3 minutes on each side.
Cut or flake the fish into small pieces and mix with the mushroom sauce.
Alternatively, cover the uncooked fish with the mushroom sauce and bake
in the oven preheated to 180°C (350°F) Gas 4 for about 15 minutes or until
the fish just flakes.

| ☺ | ☹ | ❄ |

Gratin of Sole

A very tasty fish recipe which is so easy to make.

MAKES 4 ADULT PORTIONS

4 fillets of lemon sole
salt and pepper to taste
½ small lemon
100 g/4 oz wholemeal breadcrumbs

50 g/2 oz Cheddar cheese, grated
1 heaped tablespoon chopped parsley
50 g/2 oz margarine, melted

ay the fillets in a greased ovenproof dish and season with salt, pepper and lemon juice. Put the breadcrumbs, cheese and parsley in a bowl and stir in the melted margarine. Put the breadcrumb mixture on top of the fish in the dish. Place the fish under a preheated grill for about 8 minutes until the breadcrumbs have turned a golden brown and the fish is cooked.

Cod in a Cheese Sauce with Matchstick Vegetables

Cod is particularly delicious roasted in the oven, and here it is served with colourful strips of vegetables and a tasty cheese sauce.

MAKES 2 ADULT PORTIONS

½ small red pepper, cut into thin strips
½ small yellow pepper, cut into thin strips
½ onion, peeled and thinly sliced
1 small courgette, cut into matchsticks
1 tablespoon olive oil
2 x 200 g / 7 oz cod fillets, skinned

salt and pepper
15 g / ½ oz butter
15 g / ½ oz flour
250 ml / 8 fl oz milk
40 g / 1½ oz grated Gruyère cheese
40 g / 1½ oz grated mature Cheddar cheese

lace the vegetable matchsticks in a small roasting tin, drizzle over the olive oil and cook in the oven preheated to 180°C (350°F) Gas 4 for 10 minutes, turning occasionally. Season the cod with salt and pepper and place on top of the vegetables. Return to the oven and cook for a further 10 minutes.

For the sauce, melt the butter in a saucepan and stir in the flour. Cook for 1–2 minutes, then gradually whisk in the milk. Simmer for 2–3 minutes. Stir in the grated cheese until melted. Arrange the vegetables on a plate with a portion of fish on top and pour over some of the cheese sauce.

Chinese-Style Fish Fingers

This is a very quick, easy and tasty fish recipe.

MAKES 1 ADULT PORTION

*2 fillets of plaice or sole (about
150 g/5 oz), skinned
plain flour
25 g/1 oz butter*

*1 teaspoon sesame seeds
1 tablespoon finely chopped spring onion
1 tablespoon light soy sauce
2 tablespoons orange juice*

Coat the fish in flour and sauté for 2 minutes in the butter with the sesame seeds. Add the remaining ingredients and cook on a low heat for 2–3 minutes or until cooked.

Salmon and Potato Mash

A simple to prepare tasty fish recipe. You can leave out the tomato if you prefer and simply mash the potato and salmon together with the butter and milk. If you like, you could add some cooked peas.

MAKES 2 ADULT PORTIONS

*275 g/10 oz potato, peeled and chopped
150 g/5 oz salmon fillet, skinned
1 tablespoon butter*

*1 medium tomato, skinned, seeded and
chopped
1 tablespoon milk*

Put the chopped potato in the bottom of a steamer, pour over boiling water, then cover and cook for 6 minutes. Place the salmon fillet in the steamer above the potato and cover and cook for 6 minutes. Meanwhile, melt the butter and sauté the chopped tomato until mushy. Drain the potatoes and mash together with the flaked salmon and sautéed tomatoes. Stir in the milk and check the seasoning.

Grandma's Tasty Fish Pie

This is one of my mother's recipes and is a great favourite with all the family. There is never any left the next day.

MAKES 6 ADULT PORTIONS

450 g/1 lb cod or haddock fillets, skinned
salt and pepper
plain flour
1 egg, lightly beaten
100 g/4 oz fine breadcrumbs
vegetable oil
1 onion, peeled and finely chopped
1½ tablespoons olive oil
75 g/3 oz green sweet pepper, cored,
seeded and chopped
150 g/5 oz sweet red pepper, cored,

seeded and chopped
400 g/14 oz canned tomatoes
2 tablespoons tomato purée
½ teaspoon soft brown sugar

Cheese Sauce
25 g/1 oz butter
1 tablespoon plain flour
250 ml/8 fl oz milk
75 g/3 oz Cheddar cheese, grated
40 g/1½ oz Parmesan, grated

Preheat the oven to 180°C/350°F/Gas 4. Cut the fish fillets into about 12 pieces, dip in seasoned flour, then into the lightly beaten egg, and finally coat in breadcrumbs. Sauté in the vegetable oil until golden on both sides. Drain on kitchen paper.

Sauté the onion in the olive oil for 3–4 minutes. Add the peppers and cook for 5 minutes. Drain half of the juice from the tomatoes, then add the tomatoes and the remaining juice to the peppers with the tomato purée and sugar. Season to taste and cook for about 5 minutes. Mix the cooked fish with the tomato sauce and transfer to an ovenproof dish.

Make a cheese sauce with the butter, flour and milk, stirring over a low heat until smooth and thick (see page 59). Remove from the heat and stir in two-thirds of the Cheddar and Parmesan.

Pour the cheese sauce over the fish fillets. Sprinkle with the remaining grated cheese and bake in the preheated oven for about 20 minutes. Brown under a hot grill.

Kids' Kedgeree

This is a really scrummy kedgeree which would make a great family meal that is popular with kids. It's the kind of food you could eat for breakfast or supper. If you want to make a smaller amount, simply halve the quantities.

MAKES 6 ADULT PORTIONS

350 g/12 oz undyed smoked haddock
100 ml/3½ fl oz double cream
25 g/1 oz butter
1 onion, peeled and chopped
1 teaspoon mild curry paste

200 g/7 oz basmati rice, cooked
1 teaspoon lemon juice
2 tablespoons chopped parsley
2 hard-boiled eggs, chopped
salt and pepper

Place the haddock in a microwave-proof dish and pour over the cream. Cover with clingfilm, pierce a few times with the tip of a sharp knife and place in the microwave on high for 5–6 minutes. Meanwhile, in a frying pan or wok, melt the butter and sauté the onion for 8 minutes until soft. Stir in the curry paste and rice and cook for 1 minute, stirring continuously. Flake in the haddock and add the cooking liquor, lemon juice, parsley and chopped eggs. Season with salt and pepper if necessary.

Tuna or Salmon Gratin

If you keep a can of tuna or salmon in the larder, then it is easy to combine it with some leftover vegetables to make a tasty fish pie. The ingredients can be varied according to what you have available.

MAKES 5 ADULT PORTIONS

*100 g/4 oz button mushrooms, washed
and sliced
15 g/½ oz butter
100 g/4 oz frozen peas
100–175 g/4–6 oz canned tuna or
salmon
1 large tomato, skinned, seeded and
cut into chunks
1 hard-boiled egg, chopped*

Cheese Sauce
*15 g/½ oz butter
1 tablespoon plain flour
150 ml/5 fl oz milk
50 g/2 oz Cheddar cheese, grated*

Topping
*2 potatoes, peeled, boiled and mashed
with a little milk, margarine, salt and
pepper
25 g/1 oz Cheddar cheese, grated*

Fry the mushrooms in a little butter for a couple of minutes, and cook the frozen peas until just tender. Make the sauce in the usual way, with the butter, flour and milk, stirring over a gentle heat until it thickens (see page 59). Remove from the heat and stir in the grated cheese. Add the tuna or salmon, peas, mushrooms, tomato and chopped egg to the sauce. Pour this mixture into a greased ovenproof dish. Cover with mashed potato and top with grated cheese. Cook for 20 minutes in an oven preheated to 180°C (350°F) Gas 4 and brown under the grill for a couple of minutes before serving.

Tuna Tagliatelle

This is my favourite tuna recipe.

MAKES 6 ADULT PORTIONS

½ onion, peeled and finely chopped
25 g / 1 oz butter
1 tablespoon cornflour
400 g / 14 oz canned cream of tomato soup
a pinch of mixed herbs
1 tablespoon chopped parsley
260 g / 7 oz canned tuna, drained and flaked
black pepper to taste
175 g / 6 oz green tagliatelle
1 tablespoon grated Parmesan cheese

Mushroom Cheese Sauce
½ onion, peeled and finely chopped
40 g / 1½ oz butter
100 g / 4 oz mushrooms, washed and sliced
2 tablespoons plain flour
300 ml / 10 fl oz milk
100 g / 4 oz Cheddar cheese, grated

For the sauce, fry the onion in the butter until transparent, then add the sliced mushrooms and sauté for about 3 minutes. Add the flour and continue stirring the mixture all the time. When it is well mixed, add the milk gradually and cook, stirring until thickened and smooth. Remove from the heat and stir in the grated cheese.

Fry the onion in the butter until soft. Stir the cornflour into 120 ml / 4 fl oz water until dissolved, and mix with the tomato soup. Add the mixed herbs and chopped parsley and cook, stirring, over a gentle heat for 5 minutes. Mix in the flaked tuna and heat through. Season with a little black pepper.

Boil the tagliatelle in water until *al dente*, then drain. Grease a serving dish and add the tuna and tomato mixed with the pasta and then the mushroom cheese sauce. Top with grated Parmesan. Bake in an oven preheated to 180°C (350°F) Gas 4 for 20 minutes. Brown under a hot grill before serving.

Tuna Bake with Potato Crisps

What child doesn't like potato crisps? Here is a nutritious way of making them into a healthy meal.

MAKES 6 ADULT PORTIONS

200 g/7 oz penne
2 tablespoons olive oil
1 red onion, peeled and chopped
1 garlic clove, peeled and crushed
½ red pepper, seeded and finely sliced
100 g/4 oz button mushrooms, sliced
400 g/14 oz canned chopped tomatoes

1½ tablespoons tomato ketchup
1 teaspoon red wine vinegar
1 teaspoon mixed dried herbs
400 g/14 oz canned tuna in oil,
drained
150 g/5 oz Cheddar cheese, grated
1 or 2 small bags ready salted crisps

Cook the penne according to the instructions on the packet. Heat the oil in a saucepan and sauté the onion and garlic for 5 minutes. Add the pepper and mushrooms and sauté for a further 5 minutes. Stir in the chopped tomatoes, tomato ketchup, red wine vinegar and herbs. Bring to a simmer and cook for 5 minutes. Flake the tuna, add to the sauce and cook for a further 5 minutes before stirring in the drained, cooked pasta.

Transfer to an ovenproof dish. Sprinkle with the grated cheese and crush the crisps over the top. Bake in the oven preheated to 200°C (400°F) Gas 6 for 15 minutes.

CHICKEN

Chicken Casserole with Tomatoes and Peppers

An easy-to-make chicken casserole that is delicious served with rice or mashed potato.

MAKES 6 ADULT PORTIONS

6 chicken breasts, on the bone and skinned
plain flour
salt and pepper
cooking oil
2 onions, peeled and finely sliced
2 sweet peppers (red, green or yellow),
seeded and finely sliced
800 g/28 oz canned tomatoes

2 chicken stock cubes dissolved in
175 ml/6 fl oz water
1 tablespoon chopped parsley
1 tablespoon mixed herbs
1 bay leaf
450 g/1 lb button mushrooms, carefully
washed

Roll the chicken breasts in seasoned flour and fry them, turning frequently, in a little oil until golden. Meanwhile, fry the onion for 3–4 minutes in a little oil until soft, then add the chopped peppers and continue to fry for another 3 minutes. Pat off any excess fat from the cooked chicken with some kitchen paper and drain off excess oil from the pepper and onion.

Drain off the tomato juice and chop the tomatoes into pieces. Put the chicken into a large casserole, together with the onion, pepper, tomato, concentrated chicken cube stock, herbs and some seasoning. Cook in an oven preheated to 180°C (350°F) Gas 4 for 30 minutes. Add the button mushrooms and continue to cook for a further 30 minutes.

Bar-B-Q Chicken

A good marinade will transform your barbecue, tenderising the meat, as
well as adding a delicious flavour. I use a Weber Bar-B-Q, which has a
cover, enabling me to barbecue all year round, even in England. Use
900 g/2 lb breast of chicken, skinned and on the bone, with these
marinades – they also work well with beef or lamb.

MAKES 4–5 ADULT PORTIONS

Hoisin Marinade	Teriyaki Marinade
2 tablespoons soy sauce	*3 tablespoons rice wine vinegar or white*
2 tablespoons hoisin sauce	*wine vinegar*
2 tablespoons rice wine vinegar	*2 tablespoons soy sauce*
1 tablespoon honey	*1 tablespoon honey*
1 tablespoon vegetable oil	*½ tablespoon sesame oil*
½ teaspoon crushed garlic (optional)	*1 teaspoon grated ginger root (optional)*
	1 tablespoon sliced spring onion

Mix all the marinade ingredients together. Marinate the chicken for at
least 2 hours, then barbecue, basting and turning occasionally for
15–25 minutes. Dark meat takes longer to cook than white meat. Chicken
should be cooked through, but not overcooked or it will become dry. If you
are unsure about cooking meat thoroughly before the surface is charred,
cook it in a preheated oven at 200°C (400°F) Gas 6 for 25–30 minutes and
finish it on the barbecue for a few minutes to give an authentic flavour.

Chicken Satay

These barbecued chicken skewers are fun to eat and very popular with toddlers. Help your child take the meat off the skewers, then remove the skewers – they could become dangerous in the hands of exuberant toddlers.

MAKES 2 ADULT PORTIONS

2 chicken breasts, off the bone
1 small onion, peeled
1 small red sweet pepper, seeded

Marinade
2 tablespoons peanut butter
1 tablespoon chicken stock (see page 62)
1 tablespoon rice wine vinegar
1 tablespoon honey
1 tablespoon soy sauce
1 teaspoon crushed garlic (optional)
1 teaspoon sesame seeds, toasted
(optional, see page 131)

Mix together the marinade ingredients. Soak 4 bamboo skewers in water to prevent them getting scorched. Cut the chicken, onion and pepper into chunks. Leave the chicken in the marinade for at least 2 hours. Thread with the onion and pepper on to the skewers (or just use chicken). Cook under a preheated grill for about 5 minutes each side, basting occasionally. Alternatively, cook on a barbecue.

Peanuts can cause allergic reactions (see page 15).

Chicken Paprika

This dish is not very spicy, so don't be afraid to give it to young children. If you want to make it 'hot' for adults, substitute 1 teaspoon cayenne pepper for paprika. Serve with noodles or rice.

MAKES 4 ADULT PORTIONS

vegetable oil
2 onions, peeled and chopped
4 chicken breasts, on the bone and skinned
salt and pepper
plain flour
1 red and 1 green sweet pepper, seeded and cut into strips

1 dessertspoon paprika
2 large tomatoes, skinned, seeded and cut into small pieces
300 ml/10 fl oz chicken stock (see page 62)
1 tablespoon cornflour
50 ml/2 fl oz soured cream

In a heavy saucepan heat a little oil and sauté the onion until golden. Meanwhile, roll the chicken in seasoned flour then, in a separate frying pan, brown in a little oil. Drain on kitchen paper. Add the strips of pepper, a little salt and paprika to the onion, cook for 3 minutes, then add the tomatoes and the chicken stock. Cover and simmer for 5 minutes, then add the chicken and cook until tender (about 20 minutes).

Remove the chicken, take it off the bone and cut the flesh into small bite-sized pieces. Mix the cornflour with a little cold water and stir it into the sauce. Bring to the boil, stirring constantly.

Stir the soured cream into the sauce and allow it to simmer (do not let it boil) for a few minutes. Pour over the chicken.

Chicken Fillets with Mango Chutney and Apricot

This is very simple to prepare, but tastes absolutely delicious. It is a great favourite with children because of the sweet-and-sour taste.

MAKES 2 ADULT PORTIONS

2 chicken breasts, off the bone and skinned

Sauce
1 tablespoon apricot jam
1 tablespoon mango chutney
3 tablespoons mayonnaise
1 teaspoon Worcestershire sauce
1 tablespoon lemon juice

Mix all the ingredients together for the sauce. Put the chicken into a small ovenproof dish, pour over the sauce and cover the dish with aluminium foil. Bake in the oven preheated to 180°C (350°F) Gas 4 for 30 minutes.

☺ ☹

Stir-Fried Chicken with Vegetables and Noodles

Stir-fries are popular with children and make great family food. To save time you could try using a pack of ready prepared stir-fry vegetables from the supermarket and then just add a few extra favourite vegetables of your own.

MAKES 4 ADULT PORTIONS

2 skinned chicken breasts, cut into strips
1 onion, peeled and finely sliced
1 garlic clove, peeled and crushed
75 g/3 oz carrot, cut into matchsticks
75 g/3 oz baby corn, cut into quarters
75 g/3 oz broccoli, cut into florets
100 g/4 oz courgette, trimmed and cut into matchsticks
100 g/4 oz beansprouts
1 chicken stock cube dissolved in 175 ml/6 fl oz boiling water

freshly ground black pepper

Marinade
1½ tablespoons soy sauce
1 tablespoon sake
1 teaspoon sesame oil
1 tablespoon white wine vinegar
1 teaspoon soft brown sugar
1 teaspoon cornflour
100 g/4 oz fine Chinese noodles
3 tablespoons vegetable oil

Mix the marinade ingredients and marinate the chicken for at least 30 minutes. Cook the noodles according to the packet instructions, then drain and stir in a little oil to prevent them from sticking. Strain the marinade from the chicken and reserve. Heat 1 tablespoon of the oil in a wok and stir-fry the chicken for 4–6 minutes until cooked through, then set aside. Heat the remaining oil in the wok and sauté the onion and garlic for 3 minutes. Add the carrot, baby corn and broccoli and stir-fry for 3 minutes. Add the courgette and beansprouts and stir-fry for 2 minutes. Pour the chicken stock into a small saucepan and add the reserved marinade. Bring to the boil, stirring until thickened. Season with a little salt and pepper. Add the chicken and noodles to the stir-fried vegetables, pour over the sauce and heat through.

Mulligatawny Chicken

This recipe has a tomato base and a mild curry flavour that children love. It has been a family favourite since I was a child and was invented by my mother. It is best served with rice and, for special occasions, you can serve *poppadoms* as an accompaniment. They are available in most supermarkets.

MAKES 8 ADULT PORTIONS

1 chicken, cut into about 10 pieces, skinned
salt and pepper to taste
plain flour
vegetable oil
2 medium onions, peeled and chopped
6 tablespoons tomato purée
2 tablespoons mild curry powder
960 ml/1½ pints chicken stock (see page 62)

1 large or 2 small apples, cored and thinly sliced
1 small carrot, peeled and thinly sliced
2 lemon slices
75 g/3 oz sultanas
1 bay leaf
1 dessertspoon brown sugar

Coat the chicken pieces with seasoned flour. Fry in vegetable oil until golden brown. Drain on kitchen paper and place in a casserole dish.

Fry the onion in a little oil until golden, then stir in the tomato purée. Add the curry powder and continue to stir for a couple of minutes over a low heat. Stir in 2 tablespoons of flour, then pour in 300 ml/10 fl oz of the stock, mixing well.

Add the apple, carrot, lemon slices, sultanas, bay leaf and the rest of the stock. Season with brown sugar, salt and pepper. Pour the sauce over the chicken in the casserole, cover and cook for 1 hour in an oven pre-heated to 180°C (350°F) Gas 4. Remove the lemon slices and bay leaf; take the chicken off the bone and cut it into pieces.

Sesame Chicken Nuggets with Chinese Sauce

These crisp sesame-coated nuggets in a tasty sauce are very popular. They are good served with Special Fried Rice (see page 123). It's fun for children to eat these with chopsticks – you can buy plastic chopsticks that are joined together at the top and are very easy for children to use.

MAKES 12 NUGGETS

*2 chicken breasts, off the bone and
skinned
1 egg
1 tablespoon milk
a little salt and pepper
plain flour
100 g / 4 oz sesame seeds
2 tablespoons vegetable oil*

*Chinese Sauce
250 ml / 8 fl oz unsalted chicken stock
(see page 62)
2 teaspoons soy sauce
1 teaspoon sesame oil
1 tablespoon caster sugar
1 teaspoon cider vinegar
1 tablespoon cornflour
1 spring onion, finely sliced*

Cut each chicken breast into about six pieces. Beat the egg together with the milk and dip the nuggets into seasoned flour, then into the egg and finally coat with sesame seeds. Fry in hot oil for about 5 minutes, turning the chicken frequently, until golden brown and cooked through. Mix together all the ingredients for the sauce, apart from the spring onion, in a small saucepan. Bring to the boil and then simmer for 2–3 minutes or until thickened. Add the spring onion and pour the sauce over the chicken and heat through.

Marinated Chicken on the Griddle

I love cooking chicken, meat or fish on a griddle, and it's a very healthy way of cooking as it uses very little fat. My three children love this recipe as marinating the chicken gives it a lovely flavour and makes it more tender. Make sure the griddle is really hot before you lay the food on it.

MAKES 2 ADULT PORTIONS

2 chicken breasts
1 tablespoon olive oil

Marinade
juice of ½ lemon

1 tablespoon soy sauce
1 tablespoon honey
1 small garlic clove, peeled and sliced
2 sprigs of fresh rosemary (optional)

Score the chicken breasts 2 or 3 times with a sharp knife. Mix together all the ingredients for the marinade and marinate the chicken for at least 2 hours. Heat the griddle, brush with oil, then remove the chicken from the marinade and cook for 4–5 minutes on each side or until cooked through. Cut into strips and serve with vegetables and chips or mashed potato. Serve with colourful vegetables such as carrots, broccoli or peas.

RED MEAT

Annabel's Tasty Beefburgers

The grated apple makes these beefburgers really moist and tasty. Serve in a bun with salad and ketchup, and some oven-baked chips They are also good cooked on a barbecue in summer.

MAKES 8 BEEFBURGERS

450 g / 1 lb lean minced beef or lamb
1 onion, peeled and finely chopped
1 tablespoon chopped parsley
1 chicken stock cube, dissolved in
2 tablespoons hot water
1 apple, peeled and grated

1 teaspoon Worcestershire sauce
a pinch of brown sugar
salt and freshly ground black pepper
a little flour
vegetable oil for frying, or for brushing a griddle pan

In a mixing bowl, combine all the ingredients except for the flour and vegetable oil. With floured hands, form into 8 burgers. Brush a griddle pan with a little oil and, when hot, place 4 burgers in the pan and cook for about 5 minutes each side or until browned and cooked through. Repeat with the remaining burgers. Alternatively, fry in a little hot oil in a shallow frying pan. These are good served with onion rings. Coat the onion rings in seasoned flour and deep-fry in hot oil until crispy and golden.

Cocktail Meatballs with Tomato Sauce

This is especially nice served with spaghetti and makes a great meal for the whole family. The meatballs on their own make good finger food and can be eaten either hot or cold.

MAKES 36 SMALL MEATBALLS

450 g / 1 lb lean minced beef
1 onion, peeled and finely chopped
1 apple, peeled and grated
1 tablespoon chopped parsley
1 teaspoon Marmite mixed with a little boiling water
1 egg, beaten
salt and pepper
2 thin slices white bread
2 tablespoons milk
plain flour
50 g / 2 oz margarine

Tomato Sauce
1 onion, peeled and finely chopped
a little margarine
½ red and ½ green sweet pepper, seeded and finely chopped
400 g / 14 oz canned tomatoes, drained and chopped
2 tablespoons tomato purée
1 teaspoon red wine vinegar
1 tablespoon milk
1 tablespoon chopped basil

In a bowl, mix together the meat, chopped onion, grated apple, parsley, Marmite, beaten egg and seasoning. Trim the crust off the white bread and soak it in milk for a few minutes, then squeeze out the excess moisture. Break the bread into small pieces and add this to the minced meat. Form the mixture into small balls and roll in seasoned flour. Fry in the margarine until browned all over.

To make the tomato sauce, fry the onion in a little margarine until transparent, then add the sweet peppers and fry for another 4 minutes. Add the tomatoes, tomato purée, vinegar, milk, basil and salt and pepper. Simmer for 10–15 minutes. Put the meatballs into a covered casserole and pour over the tomato sauce. Mix well and cook in an oven preheated to 150°C (300°F) Gas 2 for 1 hour.

Shepherd's Pie

If you have any little ramekin dishes, then it is very nice to make your child his very own little shepherd's pie. Let him see it, and then spoon out of the hot dish on to his plate.

MAKES 4 ADULT PORTIONS

1 onion, peeled and finely chopped
1 red sweet pepper, seeded and finely chopped
1 tablespoon finely chopped parsley
2 tablespoons vegetable oil
450 g/1 lb lean minced beef
250 ml/8 fl oz chicken stock (see page 62)
1 teaspoon Marmite

salt and pepper
100 g/4 oz button mushrooms, washed and sliced
15 g/½ oz margarine or butter

Topping
450 g/1 lb potatoes, peeled and chopped
15 g/½ oz margarine or butter
50 ml/2 fl oz milk

Fry the chopped onion, pepper and parsley in the oil until softened. Meanwhile, in a frying pan, brown the minced meat. Put meat into a food processor for 30 seconds to make it easier to chew. Add to the pan with the onion mixture and stir in the chicken stock, Marmite and seasoning. Cook over a low heat for about 20 minutes. Meanwhile, sauté the mushrooms in the margarine or butter and add these to the meat when it is cooked.

To make the topping, boil the potatoes in salted water for about 25 minutes. When soft, mash them together with half the margarine or butter, milk and some salt and pepper. Spread over the meat either in one large dish or individual ramekins, then cook in the oven preheated to 180°C (350°F) Gas 4 for 10 minutes. Dot the top with the remaining margarine and put under a hot grill for about 3 minutes or until brown and crispy.

Mini Minute Steaks

These mini steaks with a delicious gravy and sautéed potatoes are
absolutely delicious.

MAKES 2 ADULT OR 4 CHILD PORTIONS

2 tablespoons vegetable oil
1 onion, peeled and thinly sliced
1 teaspoon caster sugar
1 tablespoon water
200 ml / 7 fl oz beef stock
1 teaspoon cornflour mixed with
1 tablespoon water

a few drops of Worcestershire sauce
1 teaspoon tomato purée
salt and pepper
350 g / 12 oz peeled potatoes
25 g / 1 oz butter
4 x 60 g / 2½ oz minute steaks (fillet or
rump), about 5 mm / ¼ inch thick

To make the gravy, heat 1 tablespoon of the vegetable oil in a frying
pan. Add the onion and cook for 7–8 minutes until just turning
golden brown. Stir in the sugar and water, increase the heat and cook
for about 1 minute until the water has evaporated. Stir in the beef stock,
cornflour mixed with 1 tablespoon water, Worcestershire sauce and tomato
purée. Season with salt and pepper. Cook, stirring, for 2–3 minutes until
thickened.

For the sautéed potatoes, cut the potatoes into large chunks, bring to the
boil in lightly salted water and cook for about 8 minutes until they are just
tender. Drain and cut into 1 cm / ½ inch thick slices. Heat the butter in a
frying pan and sauté the potatoes for 5–6 minutes, turning occasionally
until golden brown and crispy,

Heat the remaining oil in a frying pan, season the steak and fry for
1–2 minutes each side. Serve with the gravy and sautéed potatoes.

Veal Stroganoff

Veal is easier than beef for your toddler to chew. This recipe is quick and easy to make – and delicious. It is very nice as a family meal served with noodles and, to give it an authentic stroganoff taste, you can even add a dollop of soured cream.

MAKES 2 ADULT PORTIONS

cooking oil
1 onion, peeled and very finely chopped
½ red and ½ yellow sweet pepper, seeded and cut into strips
225 g / 8 oz thin veal escalope, cut into strips

salt and pepper
plain flour
300 ml / 10 fl oz chicken stock (see page 62)
175 g / 6 oz button mushrooms, washed and sliced

Heat a little oil in a frying pan and sauté the onion for 3–4 minutes. Add the strips of sweet pepper and continue to cook for 1 more minute. Roll the strips of veal in seasoned flour and cook these in the frying pan for about 3 minutes or until browned (add a little more oil if you find the veal is sticking to the pan).

Pour the chicken stock over the veal and stir in the mushrooms and some salt and pepper. Simmer, covered, for about 8 minutes.

Sticky Chops

MAKES 2 ADULT PORTIONS

4 lamb chops

Marinade
2 tablespoons tomato ketchup
1 tablespoon soy sauce

1 tablespoon runny honey
1 teaspoon lemon juice
a few drops of Worcestershire sauce
a little freshly ground black pepper

Mix together all of the ingredients for the marinade, add the lamb chops and leave to marinate for 1–2 hours at room temperature or overnight in the fridge. Place on a grill pan and grill for 4–5 minutes each side, basting with any remaining marinade.

Liver and Onion

You are doing a great job if your children enjoy liver.

MAKES 1–2 ADULT PORTIONS

½ onion, peeled and chopped
1 tablespoon finely chopped green
sweet pepper
vegetable oil

2 tablespoons chopped mushrooms
1 medium tomato, skinned, seeded
and chopped
100 g/4 oz calf's liver

Fry the chopped onion and pepper in a little oil until the onions are very brown. Add the chopped mushrooms and tomato and fry for another 2 minutes. Fry the liver for 1½ minutes each side. When the liver is cooked, cut into small pieces and cover with the vegetables.

PASTA
Spaghetti with Two-Tomato Sauce

A really good home-made tomato sauce is always popular – and it can be served with any type of pasta and maybe freshly grated Parmesan cheese.

MAKES 4 CHILD PORTIONS

3 tablespoons olive oil
1 onion, peeled and chopped
1 garlic clove, peeled and crushed
4 ripe tomatoes, skinned, seeded and
chopped
400 g/14 oz canned chopped tomatoes

pinch of sugar
1 bay leaf
2 tablespoons chopped basil
salt and pepper
250 g/9 oz spaghetti

Heat the oil in a saucepan and sauté the onion and garlic for 5–6 minutes until softened. Add the fresh and canned tomatoes, sugar, bay leaf and chopped basil, then season with salt and pepper. Bring to a simmer and cook for 20 minutes. Meanwhile, cook the spaghetti according to the packet instructions. Drain the pasta and mix with the sauce.

Bow-Ties with Gruyère and Cherry Tomatoes

This is a great favourite with my children and can be eaten either warm or cold.

MAKES 4 CHILD PORTIONS

175 g/6 oz bow-tie pasta
1 tablespoon white wine vinegar
3 tablespoons olive oil
½ teaspoon Dijon mustard (optional)
a pinch of sugar

a little salt and freshly ground black pepper
1 tablespoon snipped chives
100 g/4 oz cherry tomatoes, halved or quartered
50 g/2 oz Gruyère cheese, grated

Cook the pasta in lightly salted water according to the packet instructions. Make a vinaigrette by mixing together the vinegar, oil, mustard (if using), sugar and seasoning, then add the snipped chives. Drain the pasta and put into a bowl, then mix with the cherry tomatoes and grated Gruyère cheese. Shake the vinaigrette, pour over the pasta and toss well to coat.

Macaroni Cheese with Ketchup

This tasty macaroni cheese has a lovely crunchy topping.

MAKES 4 CHILD PORTIONS

100 g/4 oz macaroni
salt
15 g/½ oz margarine
1 tablespoon plain flour
175 ml/6 fl oz milk
25 g/1 oz Cheddar cheese, grated
1 tablespoon tomato ketchup

1 dessertspoon snipped chives (optional)

Topping
2 tablespoons wholemeal breadcrumbs
25 g/1 oz Cheddar cheese, grated
a little margarine

Cook the macaroni in boiling salted water according to the instructions on the packet. Use the margarine, flour and milk to make a thick white sauce (see page 59). Remove from the heat and stir in the cheese, tomato ketchup and chives, if using.

Put the macaroni into an ovenproof dish and mix with the sauce. Sprinkle with the breadcrumbs and grated cheese and dot with margarine. Brown under the grill for 2–3 minutes to make a crispy topping.

Spaghetti Primavera

Spaghetti with vegetables makes a delicious and colourful dish. Be careful not to overcook the vegetables or they will be soft and mushy.

MAKES 4 CHILD PORTIONS

100 g / 4 oz mushrooms, washed and sliced
40 g / 1½ oz butter
1 tablespoon flour
150 ml / 5 fl oz vegetable stock (see page 33)
4 medium tomatoes (about 225 g / 8 oz), skinned, seeded and chopped
1 tablespoon torn fresh basil

2 tablespoons milk
salt and pepper
100 g / 4 oz each broccoli and cauliflower, broken into small florets
1 medium courgette, trimmed and cut into matchsticks
150 g / 5 oz spaghettini or tagliolini
Parmesan cheese, freshly grated (optional)

Sauté the mushrooms in butter for 3 minutes. Stir in the flour and cook for half a minute. Gradually stir in the stock over a gentle heat, stirring, until the sauce becomes smooth and thick. Add the chopped tomatoes, basil and milk and cook for about 4 minutes. Season to taste. Meanwhile, lightly season the broccoli, cauliflower and courgette and steam until just tender (about 5 minutes). Cook the pasta according to the packet. Toss together with the sauce and steamed vegetables. Sprinkle with Parmesan cheese if you like.

Bow-Ties with Tomato and Mozzarella Sauce

A very tasty easy to prepare tomato sauce enriched with two cheeses.

MAKES 4 CHILD PORTIONS

150 g/5 oz bow-tie pasta
2 tablespoons olive oil
1 onion, peeled and chopped
1 garlic clove, peeled and crushed
400 g/14 oz canned chopped tomatoes
1 teaspoon balsamic vinegar

a pinch of sugar
1 tablespoon torn basil leaves
100 ml/3½ fl oz vegetable stock
100 g/4 oz mozzarella, diced
3 tablespoons grated Parmesan cheese

Cook the pasta according to the packet directions. To make the sauce, heat the olive oil in a pan and sauté the onion and garlic for 5–6 minutes until softened. Stir in the chopped tomatoes, balsamic vinegar, sugar, basil and stock and simmer for 10 minutes. Stir in the mozzarella and Parmesan cheese. Season to taste and mix with the bow-tie pasta.

Animal Pasta Salad with Multicoloured Vegetables

I make this recipe with multicoloured animal-shaped pasta. Toddlers love picking out all the different ingredients. It looks very attractive and colourful on a plate and can be served warm or cold. You can omit the chicken for a vegetarian dish.

MAKES 4 CHILD PORTIONS

100 g/4 oz multicoloured pasta shapes
1 chicken breast, skinned and cut into bite-sized pieces
vegetable oil
3 baby carrots or 1 medium carrot, cut into fine strips
100 g/4 oz button mushrooms, washed and sliced
50 g/2 oz each broccoli and cauliflower, broken into small florets
3 courgettes, trimmed and sliced
50 g/2 oz French beans, chopped

100 g/4 oz frozen sweetcorn
½ red sweet pepper, finely chopped
salt
sugar

Dressing
2 tablespoons cider vinegar or red wine vinegar
salt and black pepper
50 ml/2 fl oz olive oil
2 spring onions, finely sliced, or 2 tablespoons snipped chives

Cook the pasta according to the packet instructions and drain. Fry the chicken in a little oil for 2 minutes, then add the carrots and mushrooms and continue to cook for a further 5 minutes. Meanwhile steam the broccoli, cauliflower, courgettes and beans until cooked but still crisp. The broccoli and cauliflower will need a little longer than the courgettes and beans. Cook the sweetcorn and red pepper in water with a little salt and sugar for 5 minutes.

To prepare the dressing, whisk the vinegar with salt and pepper, then whisk in the olive oil a little at a time. Add the spring onions. Combine all the ingredients together and pour the dressing over.

FRUIT AND DESSERTS

Poached Fruits

MAKES 4 ADULT PORTIONS

2 large or 3 small pears, peeled,
quartered and cored
150 g/5 oz plums, halved and stoned
150 g/5 oz blackberries

75 ml/3 fl oz apple juice
60 g/2½ oz caster sugar
1 small stick cinnamon
100 g/4 oz raspberries

Cut the pear quarters in half and place in a large saucepan. Add plums, blackberries, apple juice, caster sugar and the cinnamon stick. Bring to a gentle simmer and cover with a lid for 10 minutes. Stir in the raspberries. Remove the cinnamon stick before serving and serve chilled.

Peach Melba Delight

A healthy alternative to this favourite ice-cream dessert.

MAKES 1 ADULT PORTION

100 g/4 oz raspberries, fresh or frozen
2 teaspoons caster sugar
1 small carton mild natural yoghurt

1 ripe peach, skinned, stoned and cut
into small pieces

Put the raspberries and sugar in a small saucepan and cook gently for 2–3 minutes or until soft and mushy. Press the raspberries through a sieve and mix together with the yoghurt and chopped peach.

Snow-Covered Fruit Salad

Try this combination of fruits, which are all rich in Vitamin C – better than any vitamin tablets. You can make your own combination according to what is in season.

MAKES 5 ADULT PORTIONS

1 peach, skinned, stoned and cut into small pieces
1 papaya, peeled, seeded and cut into small chunks
8 strawberries, hulled and cut into quarters
2 oranges, peeled, pith removed and cut into chunks
1 tablespoon raspberries or blackberries
½ small cantaloupe melon, flesh removed and cut into chunks

100 g/4 oz cherries, stoned and halved
1 small wedge of watermelon, flesh removed and cut into chunks
2 kiwi fruit, peeled and sliced
juice of 1 orange

Topping
450 ml/15 fl oz natural yoghurt
2 tablespoons honey
2 tablespoons wheatgerm or muesli (optional)

Combine all the fruits together in a large bowl. Pour the orange juice over them and mix well.

Mix the yoghurt with the honey and wheatgerm or muesli, if using, and pour over the fruit just before serving.

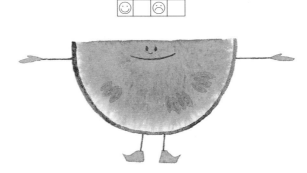

Peaches with Amaretto Biscuits

Amaretto biscuits are small round macaroons from Italy which can be bought in most supermarkets. This delicious fruit dessert can be made with many different fruits. Try a combination of white peaches and raspberries or sliced plums. You could also make this dessert using light crème fraîche.

MAKES 2 ADULT PORTIONS

2 large ripe peaches, stoned and sliced
25 g / 1 oz crushed amaretto biscuits

125 ml / 4½ fl oz crème fraîche
1 heaped tablespoon brown sugar

Place the sliced peaches in a shallow ovenproof dish and sprinkle with the crushed amaretto biscuits. Cover with the crème fraîche and then sprinkle over the brown sugar. Place under a preheated grill for about 6 minutes until golden.

Pear, Apple and Raspberry Crumble

A really good crumble bursting with fruit is comfort food at its very best;
and it is easy to prepare and always a great favourite with the family. I
like to choose fruits that have a slightly tart flavour. Rhubarb with
50 g/2 oz brown sugar and a few tablespoons of orange juice makes a
good fruit crumble, and the apple and blackberry mixture on page 86
mixed with 100 g/4 oz light muscovado sugar is also delicious. Crumbles
are best served hot with custard or vanilla ice cream.

MAKES 6 ADULT PORTIONS

2 eating apples, peeled and chopped
2 ripe pears, peeled and chopped
250 g/9 oz raspberries, fresh or frozen
1 tablespoon caster sugar

Crumble Topping
150 g/5 oz plain flour
a pinch of salt
100 g/4 oz cold butter, cut into pieces
75 g/3 oz soft brown sugar
50 g/2 oz rolled oats

To make the crumble topping, mix together the flour and salt and rub
in the butter with your fingers to resemble breadcrumbs. Stir in the
sugar and oats.

Mix together the apples, pears and raspberries in a suitable ovenproof
dish (I use a 25 x 20 cm/10 x 8 inch oval dish), sprinkle over the sugar and
top with the crumble mixture. Bake in an oven preheated to 200°C (400°F)
Gas 6 for 30–35 minutes, by which time the top of the crumble should
have turned a golden brown.

American-Style Cheesecake

This is one of the most delicious cheesecakes I have ever tasted. Serve it
plain or with the cherry topping.

MAKES 10 ADULT PORTIONS

Base
250 g / 9 oz digestive biscuits
125 g / 4½ oz butter

Filling
225 g / 8 oz caster sugar
3 tablespoons cornflour
675 g / 1½ lb cream cheese, eg.
Philadelphia

2 eggs
1 teaspoon vanilla essence or grated zest
of ½ lemon
300 ml / 10 fl oz whipping cream
75 g / 3 oz sultanas (optional)

Topping
425 g / 15 oz canned cherries in syrup
½ tablespoon cornflour

To make the base, break the biscuits into pieces, put them in a plastic
bag and crush with a rolling pin. Melt the butter and stir in the
crushed biscuits. Line a 23 cm/9 inch springform cake tin with baking
paper and grease the sides. Press the crushed biscuit mixture over the base.

For the filling, mix the sugar and cornflour. Beat in the cream cheese.
Add the eggs and vanilla (or lemon zest). Beat until smooth. Slowly whisk
in the cream until thickened. Stir in the sultanas. Pour over the biscuit base.
Bake for 1 hour in an oven preheated
to 180°C (350°F) Gas 4. Cool.

For the topping, drain the cherries,
reserving 120 ml/4 fl oz syrup. Mix the
cornflour with 1 tablespoon syrup.
Pour the remaining syrup into a pan,
stir in the cornflour mixture and bring
to the boil, stirring until thick. Cool.
Decorate the cheesecake with circles of
cherries and pour over the glaze.

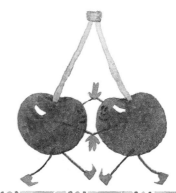

Iced Lollies

Iced lollies are always popular with children. You can buy lolly moulds with reusable plastic sticks. Fill the moulds with your chosen fruit purée or fruit juice, put the plastic sticks on top (these also serve as covers) and freeze on a level surface in the freezer. Dip the mould into warm water when you want to get an iced lolly out.

You can make your own fruit purées from fresh fruits in season or you can use natural fruit juices as the basis of your lollies. Experiment with different combinations like puréed and sieved berry fruits sweetened with a little icing sugar mixed with blackcurrant juice, and stir in natural or fruit-flavoured yoghurt for a frozen-yoghurt lolly. These pure ingredients are much better for your child than commercial iced lollies, many of which are full of additives, colourings and sugar.

My son Nicholas, when two years old, had fairly sophisticated taste and developed a penchant for passion-fruit ice lollies (as did his father, who goes straight for the freezer after supper!). Try also cranberry and raspberry juice or puréed tinned lychees.

Two-tone iced lollies are fun. Half-fill the moulds with purée or juice of one colour, freeze, then pour over a purée of a contrasting colour.

Peach and Passion-Fruit Lollies

MAKES 6 ICED LOLLIES

2 large oranges, squeezed
strained juice of 3 passion fruit

2 juicy ripe peaches, skinned, stoned and
chopped

Combine all the ingredients in a blender or processor and blend until smooth. Pour into iced-lolly moulds and freeze.

Annabel's Bread and Butter Pudding

This is the perfect pudding for when the cupboard is pretty bare. It is also delicious made with raisin bread, cholla or sliced panettone cake.

MAKES 5 ADULT PORTIONS

250 ml/8 fl oz milk
250 ml/8 fl oz whipping cream
1 split vanilla pod
4 thin slices white bread, crusts removed
butter for spreading

50 g/2 oz sultanas
25 g/1 oz raisins
3 eggs
50 g/2 oz caster sugar
2 tablespoons apricot jam

Slowly boil the milk and cream in a saucepan with the vanilla pod, then remove from the heat. Stand for 10 minutes, then sieve. Spread the bread with butter and cut each slice into four triangles. Arrange in a greased oven-proof dish (about 25 x 20 cm/10 x 8 inches) with the sultanas and raisins between the slices. Whisk the eggs with the sugar, then gradually mix in the milk and cream. Pour over the bread and bake in an oven preheated to 160°C (325°F) Gas 3 for 45–50 minutes. Remove and allow to cool a little. Gently heat the jam, with a little water, strain and brush over the pudding.

Grandma's Lokshen Pudding

Lokshen is vermicelli: very fine egg noodles.

MAKES 4 ADULT PORTIONS

225 g/8 oz vermicelli
1 large egg, beaten
25 g/1 oz butter, melted
250 ml/8 fl oz milk

1 tablespoon vanilla sugar or caster sugar
½ teaspoon mixed spice
75 g/3 oz each sultanas and raisins
a few flaked almonds (optional)

Cook the vermicelli in boiling water for about 5 minutes. Drain and mix with the remaining ingredients. Place in a greased, shallow baking dish, and bake at 180°C (350°F) Gas 4 for about 30 minutes.

Frozen Strawberry Yoghurt
Ice Cream

A delicious easy-to-make frozen-yoghurt ice cream using only natural ingredients. You can also make a peach melba frozen yoghurt using fresh raspberries, puréed and sieved, and peach yoghurt. I like to serve this as a Knickerbocker Glory in a tall glass with fresh berries.

MAKES 6 ADULT PORTIONS

100 g/4 oz caster sugar
350 g/12 oz fresh strawberries
300 ml/10 fl oz strawberry yoghurt

150 ml/5 fl oz double cream, whipped
1 egg white, whisked

Put the sugar in a saucepan with 300 ml/10 fl oz water, bring to the boil and continue to boil for 5 minutes to make a syrup. Set aside to cool for a few minutes. Purée the strawberries, then mix with the syrup and stir in the yoghurt and whipped cream. Churn for 10 minutes in an ice cream-making machine, then fold in the whipped egg white and churn for another 10 minutes or until firm.

This can also be made without an ice-cream-making machine but it will be more time-consuming. Pour the mixture into a plastic container and freeze. Remove and whisk when semi-frozen, then return to the freezer. Whisk again after 1 hour, fold in the whipped egg white, freeze again and whisk two more times during the freezing process.

BAKING FOR TODDLERS
Funny Shape Biscuits

These biscuits contain no sugar and are ideal for babies who are teething. Biscuit cutters come in all sorts of weird and wonderful shapes. I use a gingerbread-man cutter and animal cut-outs and my son can't wait to get his hands on the biscuits. I get a running commentary as to which piece of the anatomy he has just eaten!

MAKES 15–20 BISCUITS (DEPENDING ON SIZE OF CUTTERS)

50 g/2 oz wholemeal flour
100 g/4 oz plain white flour
75 g/3 oz semolina
¼ teaspoon each ground ginger,
cinnamon and salt
75 g/3 oz margarine or butter

1 medium ripe banana
2 tablespoons maple syrup
1 egg, lightly beaten
cream cheese for spreading (optional)
a few raisins (optional)

Put the flours, semolina, ginger, cinnamon and salt into a mixing bowl and rub in the margarine or butter. Mash the banana well with the maple syrup and stir into the mixture to make a smooth pliable dough.

Roll out on lightly floured surface and cut into shapes with biscuit cutters. Brush with the beaten egg and bake on lightly greased baking trays in an oven preheated to 200°C (400°F) Gas 6 for 20 minutes until golden and firm. Cool on a wire rack.

If you wish, spread the cooled biscuits with cream cheese, marking with a fork to represent the animals' fur. Use pieces of raisin for eyes and noses.

Apple Flowers

You can use ready-rolled sheets of puff pastry which only need to be unrolled and baked – so it couldn't be simpler to make these delicious pastries. Alternatively, use a block of puff pastry and roll it out yourself.

MAKES 6 MINI APPLE TARTS

300 g/11 oz puff pastry
40 g/1½ oz butter
40 g/1½ oz caster sugar
1 egg
a few drops of almond essence
50 g/2 oz ground almonds

25 g/1 oz melted butter
3 small eating apples
caster sugar for sprinkling
2 tablespoons apricot jam
1 tablespoon lemon juice
6 glacé cherries

Preheat the oven to 200°C (400°F) Gas 6. Cut 6 circles out of the pastry using a round pastry cutter (approx. 10 cm/4 inches) or cut around a plate using a sharp knife. To make the almond filling, cream together the butter and sugar until soft, then beat in the egg, a few drops of almond essence and the ground almonds to make a smooth cream. Prick the pastry a few times with a fork and brush with a little melted butter. Spread some of the almond cream over each of the circles.

Peel and core the apples, then cut in half and slice thinly. Arrange the sliced fruit in circles on the pastry rounds. Brush with a little melted butter, sprinkle over some caster sugar and bake in the preheated oven for about 20 minutes or until the pastry is crisp and the fruit is cooked. Transfer the tarts to a wire rack to cool.

Warm the jam and lemon juice in a small saucepan and then brush the fruit with a little of the melted, sieved apricot jam to glaze the tarts. Decorate the centre of each tart with a glacé cherry.

Smartie Fairy Cakes

These little cakes can be frozen, which is best done before they are iced.
They are ideal for a birthday celebration and it's fun to decorate them
with faces using sweets and tubes of writing icing.

MAKES 12 CAKES

100 g/4 oz soft margarine
100 g/4 oz caster sugar
2 eggs
100 g/4 oz self-raising flour
1 teaspoon vanilla essence

Cream-Cheese Icing
50 g/2 oz unsalted butter
225 g/8 oz icing sugar, sieved
1 teaspoon vanilla essence
100 g/4 oz cream cheese

Glacé Icing
225g/8 oz icing sugar, sieved
about 2 tablespoons water
a few drops of food colouring

Decoration
*1 packet candy-coated chocolate
beans (Smarties)*
1 packet dolly mixtures
*assorted colours of writing icing
in tubes*

Chocolate Icing
50 g/2 oz soft unsalted butter
75 g/3 oz icing sugar, sieved
1 tablespoon cocoa powder

Cream the margarine and sugar together until light and fluffy, then beat
in the eggs one at a time together with 1 tablespoon of the flour. Add
the vanilla essence and fold in the remaining flour. Line a bun tin with paper
cases and half-fill each case with the mixture. Bake in an oven preheated
to 180°C (350°F) Gas 4 for 20 minutes. Remove and cool on a wire rack.

I like to make two different coloured icings, so I use chocolate and then a
pale cream-cheese icing. If you prefer, make a simple glacé icing. Mix the
icing sugar with enough water to form a spreading consistency, then divide
into two before you stir in the colouring, using different colours for each half.

For the chocolate icing, cut the butter into small pieces and beat it in a
bowl with a wooden spoon until creamy. Beat the sugar a little at a time
into the butter, then beat in the cocoa powder.

For the cream-cheese icing, beat the butter, sugar and vanilla essence until crumbly. Stir in the cream cheese. Do not over-beat or it will become watery. Spread over the cakes.

Ice and decorate the cakes with funny faces.

Pineapple and Raisin Muffins

These are absolutely delicious, and very healthy too; they never last long in our house!

MAKES ABOUT 13 MUFFINS

100 g / 4 oz plain flour
100 g / 4 oz plain wholemeal flour
1 teaspoon baking powder
¾ teaspoon bicarbonate of soda
1 teaspoon ground cinnamon
1 teaspoon ground ginger
½ teaspoon salt

175 ml / 6 fl oz vegetable oil
75 g / 3 oz castor sugar
2 eggs
125 g / 4½ oz grated carrots
225 g / 8 oz canned crushed pineapple, drained
100 g / 4 oz raisins

Preheat the oven to 180°C (350°F) Gas 4. Sift together the flours, baking powder, bicarbonate of soda, cinnamon, ginger and salt and mix well. Beat the oil, sugar and eggs together until well blended. Add the grated carrots, crushed pineapple and raisins. Gradually add the flour mixture, beating just enough to combine all the ingredients.

Pour the batter into muffin trays lined with paper cases and bake for about 25 minutes or until golden. (These can be cooked in fairy-cake trays, but you will need to reduce the cooking time.) Cool on a wire rack.

Yoghurt Magimix Cake

This cake has a lovely flavour and a very moist texture. It takes no more than 5 minutes to prepare. You can also make it in two sandwich tins. Beat 250 ml/8 fl oz double cream with 25 g/1 oz caster sugar and fold in 100 g/4 oz raspberries, and use this to sandwich the two cakes together.

MAKES 8 ADULT PORTIONS

160 g/5¼ oz caster sugar　　*225 g/8 oz plain flour*
250 ml/8 fl oz vegetable oil　　*3 teaspoons baking powder*
225 ml/8 fl oz natural set yoghurt　　*2 teaspoons vanilla essence*
2 eggs　　*icing sugar*

Grease a 25 cm/10 in round chiffon cake tin. In a blender or food processor, mix the sugar with the oil, then add the yoghurt and mix. Blend with the eggs, flour, baking powder and vanilla essence. Pour into the prepared tin and bake at 160°C (325°F) Gas 3 for about 50 minutes. Sift icing sugar over the top when cold.

White-Chocolate-Button Cookies

These are so easy to make and are really delicious. Baked for only 12 minutes, they should be quite soft when they are taken out of the oven so that when they cool down they are lovely and moist.

MAKES 20 COOKIES

100 g/4 oz unsalted butter or　　*175 g/6 oz plain flour*
margarine at room temperature　　*½ teaspoon baking powder*
100 g/4 oz caster sugar　　*¼ teaspoon salt*
100 g/4 oz brown sugar　　*175 g/6 oz white chocolate buttons*
1 egg　　*75 g/3 oz pecans or walnuts, chopped*
1 teaspoon vanilla essence　　*(optional)*

Beat the butter or margarine together with the sugars. With a fork, beat the egg together with the vanilla and add this to the butter mixture.

In a bowl, mix together the flour, baking powder and salt. Add this to the butter and egg mixture and blend well.

Break the chocolate buttons into smaller pieces with a rolling pin or in a food processor, and stir these, together with the nuts (if used), into the mixture.

Line several baking sheets with non-stick baking paper and roll the dough into walnut-sized balls. Put these on to the sheets, spaced well apart, and bake in an oven preheated to 190°C (375°F) Gas 5 for 12 minutes. Take carefully off the baking paper and let them cool.

Chocolate Muesli and Rice Krispie Squares

These will be a tasty treat for your child and they are very quick and easy to prepare.

MAKES 16 SQUARES

150 g/5 oz muesli (your child's favourite type)
50 g/2 oz Rice Krispies
50 g/2 oz dried apricots, chopped

100 g/4 oz butter
6 tablespoons golden syrup
50 g/2 oz plain chocolate, broken into pieces

Combine the muesli, Rice Krispies and dried apricots. Put the butter and golden syrup in a saucepan and heat gently. Add the chocolate pieces and stir until melted. Stir the chocolate and syrup mixture into the dry ingredients until well coated. Press the mixture firmly into a greased 20 cm /8 inch square shallow tin, using a potato masher to level the surface. Put in the fridge to set when cool, then cut into squares.

Traditional English Fruit Cake

I like to make several of these dark rich fruit cakes with my children a month before Christmas as presents for teachers, family and friends. We decorate them and put them in fancy cake tins; they will keep well for several months. If making this for adults, soak the fruit in brandy and port instead of orange juice – it tastes wonderful. For added flavour, make holes in the cake with a skewer and add extra brandy and port after the cake is cooked.

MAKES 16 ADULT PORTIONS

150 ml/5 fl oz orange juice or
4 tablespoons each brandy and port
275 g/10 oz each currants and sultanas
350 g/12 oz raisins
225 g/8 oz plain flour
1 teaspoon baking powder
½ teaspoon salt
2 teaspoons powdered cinnamon
1 teaspoon ground ginger
2 teaspoons mixed spice

225 g/8 oz butter
150 g/5 oz brown sugar
4 eggs
150 g/5 oz mixed peel
100 g/4 oz glacé cherries, chopped
100 g/4 oz pecans or walnuts, chopped
100 g/4 oz apricot jam
3 tablespoons water
extra pecans or walnuts and glacé fruits
for decoration

Pour the orange juice over the dried fruit and leave to soak overnight. Sift together the flour, baking powder, salt and spices. Cream the butter with the sugar. Beat in the eggs, one at a time, with 1 tablespoon of the flour mixture. Stir in the remaining flour mixture and the dried fruit, peel, cherries and nuts. Line the base of a 25 cm/10 inch round cake tin and grease the sides. Pour in the cake mix. Bake in a preheated oven at 150°C (300°F) Gas 2 for 2–2½ hours. If the top is getting too brown, cover with greaseproof paper. When cooked, a skewer inserted into the centre of the cake should come out clean. Cool in the tin for 30 minutes. Turn out on to a wire rack to cool thoroughly. Wrap in foil and store in a cool dry place.

Warm the jam and water and press through a sieve. Brush the top of the cake with some glaze and decorate with the fruit and nuts. Brush with the remaining glaze.

Cheese Pretzels

These are delicious and great fun to make. Your children will enjoy helping you twist the pretzels into different shapes. You can even make letters of the alphabet and spell your child's name.

MAKES 20 PRETZELS

1 sachet dried yeast
225 ml/8 fl oz warm water
350 g/12 oz plain flour
½ teaspoon salt

150 g/5 oz Gruyère or Cheddar cheese,
grated
2 tablespoons vegetable oil
1 tablespoon sea salt
1 tablespoon sesame seeds

Dissolve the yeast in the warm water. Sift the flour and salt into a large bowl and stir in the cheese, oil and yeast liquid. Bring together to form a dough and knead on a floured surface for 10 minutes by hand, or for 5 minutes using a dough hook. Place in an oiled bowl, cover with clingfilm and leave in a warm place for about 1 hour. Break off small pieces of dough, roll into 25 cm/10 inch long strands and twist into pretzel shapes. Arrange on a greased baking tray. Brush with oil and sprinkle some with sea salt and some with sesame seeds. Bake in an oven preheated to 200°C (400°F) Gas 6 for 15 minutes until golden brown.

HEALTHY SNACKS

Fruit Snacks

Wash fruit well. Peel, core, seed or stone and trim as needed.

Bananas, whole or cut into pieces

Chunks of peeled and cored apples

Chunks of pear

Orange, mandarin or clementine segments with as much of the pith removed as possible (make sure there are no pips in the fruit)

Kiwi fruit, peeled and sliced

Strawberries, hulled and halved

Seedless grapes, skinned for babies under one year

Melon, peeled and cut into bite-sized pieces

Peaches, skinned and sliced

Mango, peeled and sliced

Papaya, peeled, seeded and cut in thick slices

Raspberries, carefully washed

Lychees, peeled and stoned (toddlers can easily choke on lychee stones)

Pineapple, peeled and cut into chunks

Dried fruit such as apricots, prunes, raisins (if too tough, soak in boiling water)

Chocolate-Dipped Fruit

A very appealing way of giving fruit to children is to melt some dark chocolate in a double boiler (or in a microwave), dip the tip of the fruit piece into the chocolate and pierce the fruit with a cocktail stick. Stick the cocktail sticks with the fruit into an orange and put this into the fridge to allow the chocolate to harden. Strawberries, pineapple chunks and orange or tangerine segments are especially nice. Remember to remove the cocktail sticks before giving the fruit to your child.

Whole bananas can be coated in chocolate. Place on waxed paper and freeze or chill until the chocolate has set.

If you are worried about your child having too much chocolate, use carob as a substitute.

SNACKS THAT WON'T HARM YOUR CHILD'S TEETH

Vegetable Snacks

As with fruit, wash, peel, trim and seed as appropriate.

Toddlers love to dip raw vegetables into a sauce, and a nicely arranged selection of crudités is great for a toddler who is teething. Try some of the simple but delicious dip recipes that follow. Think also about things like *hummous* – made from chickpeas and which can be bought in most supermarkets – or cream cheese mixed with a little sour cream, chives and seasoning, which makes a nice creamy dip.

Carrots and cabbage, grated or chopped, mixed with a little mayonnaise and raisins, makes a simple and nutritious snack piled on to lettuce leaves.

Cheese Snacks

Cheese makes an ideal snack for toddlers. Try using a cookie cutter to make animal shapes from slices of cheese. Edam, Gruyère and Emmenthal are particular favourites with most children. Individual cheeses like the small round Babybel and the wrapped triangles of cheese are ideal as well.

Cottage cheese is also popular, plain or simply mixed with something like chopped pineapple. You could also make a scoopful of cheese into a ball, accompany it with a scoopful of grated apple mixed with raisins, and surround it with a selection of mixed fruit chopped very small. This makes a nutritious, yet delicious, snack.

Green Goddess Dip

Serve this tasty dip surrounded by a selection of raw vegetable sticks like carrots, cucumber, red pepper and celery. Add some cherry tomatoes, corn chips and bread sticks for a popular and nutritious snack.

MAKES 2 ADULT PORTIONS

1 large ripe avocado
½ tablespoon fresh lemon juice
2 tablespoons cream cheese
1 tablespoon sliced spring onion

2 tomatoes, skinned, seeded and finely chopped
1 tablespoon diced red sweet pepper
salt and pepper to taste

Cut the avocado in half, stone and scoop the flesh out of the skin. Mash it together with the rest of the ingredients. This will turn brown if left standing for too long.

Chef's Salad with Turkey and Cheese

Toddlers will enjoy eating mini salads like this one.

MAKES 3 CHILD PORTIONS

1 baby gem lettuce, cut into small pieces
2 tomatoes, skinned and quartered
75 g / 3 oz Edam cheese, cubed
100 g / 4 oz cooked turkey or chicken, diced

1 chunk cucumber, peeled and diced
1 spring onion, finely sliced
1½ tablespoons mayonnaise
½ teaspoon white wine vinegar
¼ tub salad cress

Place the baby gem lettuce in a serving dish and sprinkle over the tomatoes, Edam, turkey or chicken and cucumber. Mix together the sliced spring onions, mayonnaise and white wine vinegar. Toss the salad in this dressing and sprinkle over the salad cress.

Home-Made Fast-Food Pizza

These delicious easy-to-make pizzas are always popular. If you prefer, you can use crumpets or small baguettes cut in half as an alternative to the muffin bases.

MAKES 4 MINI PIZZAS

1 spring onion, finely sliced
4 button mushrooms, washed and sliced
15 g/½ oz butter
2 tomatoes, skinned, seeded and chopped
1 dessertspoon tomato purée

1 dessertspoon chopped fresh basil
50 g/2 oz frozen sweetcorn
a little freshly ground black pepper
2 muffins, split in half
40 g/1½ oz Cheddar cheese, grated

Sauté the spring onion and mushrooms in the butter for 2 minutes. Stir in the tomatoes, tomato purée and basil and cook for 2 minutes more. Cook the sweetcorn according to the instructions on the packet, combine it with the tomato mixture and season with a little pepper. Heat the grill and toast the split muffins for a few minutes. Top with the tomato and sweetcorn mixture, sprinkle with the grated cheese and grill until the cheese is bubbling and golden.

Stuffed Eggs

Cut hard-boiled eggs in half lengthwise and cut a thin sliver off the base
of each half so that they stand firm. Finely mash the yolks with one of
the following, and fill the hollow. Remember that the hollow of a boiled
egg is quite small, so you do not need a lot of filling.

*chopped cucumber, lettuce, tomato, and
mayonnaise*
OR
cottage cheese and chives
OR
poached salmon and mayonnaise

OR
*finely chopped chicken and tomato
ketchup*
OR
*canned salmon or tuna, mayonnaise and
chopped spring onion*

Top-Hat Egg

This is a great snack or breakfast treat for children and they'll have fun
helping you make it. You could also use cookie cutters to cut out shapes
like a heart or an animal in the centre of the bread.

MAKES 1 ADULT PORTION

1 thick slice bread
15 g/½ oz butter

1 egg yolk
salt and pepper

Press out a circle from the centre of the bread using a pastry cutter of
about 7.5 cm/3 inch diameter. Butter both sides of the bread and fry
on one side for about 1 minute in a small frying pan. Flip the bread over,
place a knob of butter in the hole and allow it to sizzle. Crack the egg into
the hole, season lightly and cook, covered, for about 4 minutes or until set.
Serve with the circle of fried bread over the egg.

French Toast with Marmite

This recipe makes excellent finger food for your toddler and can be served with boiled or scrambled egg to make a complete meal.

MAKES 1 ADULT PORTION

½ teaspoon Marmite
1 slice wholemeal bread

1 egg
a little butter or margarine

Thinly spread the Marmite on both sides of the bread. Beat the egg and pour it on to a flat plate. Soak the bread in the egg. Meanwhile, melt a little butter in a frying pan, then fry the bread until golden on both sides. Cut the bread into 'soldiers', removing the crusts if your child prefers.

Sandwiches

Sandwiches can come in all shapes and sizes. Try making animal-shaped sandwiches by cutting them out with a cookie cutter. Pinwheel sandwiches are very appealing too (see page 186).

Toasted sandwiches are a meal in themselves. It is well worth investing in a toasted sandwich maker that seals the bread.

Try using lots of different types of bread: small round pitta bread, slit and stuffed with salad; raisin bread; open sandwiches on bridge rolls; bagels (these are excellent for a toddler to chew on when he is teething); pumpernickel bread (which is black); French bread; or even simply make a sandwich where one side is white bread and one side is brown.

Presentation is very important. A child is far more likely to eat something that looks appealing. Sprinkle the sandwiches with salad cress, decorate with thinly serrated vegetables or make your sandwiches into little trains or boats. It doesn't take long and it's fun to do. I think you will find that a lot of toddlers will reach out for your sandwiches.

On the following pages are some suggestions for sandwich fillings. Your toddler will soon let you know his preferences!

Pinwheel Sandwiches

Remove the crusts from two slices of bread. Place them on a board, overlapping the edges slightly, and then roll them together with a rolling pin to join the slices together and gently flatten the bread, making it more pliable. Alternatively, cut the crust from the side of a long rectangular dense-textured loaf, and cut into long thin slices – this way you can prepare pinwheels without any join. Spread evenly with butter or margarine and the desired filling, and roll up the bread like a Swiss roll. Cut into slices to make little pinwheels. It is a good idea to prepare these in advance, wrap them in cling film and set aside in the fridge – they will slice better if chilled first.

You can even make a variegated pinwheel sandwich by rolling one brown and one white slice of bread (spread with different but complementary fillings) together.

Chocolate spread and banana
Peanut butter and raspberry jam
Peanut butter and mashed banana
Cream cheese with avocado or
   cooked spinach
Cream cheese, Marmite and
   shredded lettuce

Peanuts can cause allergic reactions (see page 15).

Cream cheese and crushed pineapple (or fruit purée)

Cream or curd cheese, toasted sesame seeds, and mustard and cress

Cream cheese and cucumber

Cream cheese and crushed cornflakes

Cream cheese and strawberry jam in raisin bread

Cream cheese with slices of smoked salmon in a bagel

Cream cheese with chopped dried apricots

Cream cheese and redcurrant jelly

Cottage cheese with avocado and lemon juice

Cheese and chutney

Grated cheese with grated apple and pear

Plain fromage frais and raisins

Taramasalata

Sliced falafel with grated carrots and raisins

Chopped hard-boiled egg, watercress and mayonnaise

Egg mayonnaise with a little curry powder

Chopped hard-boiled egg with mashed sardines

Tuna mayonnaise and salad cress

Tuna or salmon salad with chopped celery

Canned salmon, chopped egg and mayonnaise

Smoked salmon

Chopped chicken, mayonnaise and yoghurt with a little curry powder and raisins

Chicken or turkey with chutney

Grilled chicken liver, mashed with fried onions and hard-boiled egg

Open Toasted Sandwiches

Toast the bread, spread with the topping and cook under a hot grill.

Cheese and tomato

Diced ham and pineapple with grated cheese

Canned sardines in tomato sauce

TODDLER MEAL PLANNER

	Breakfast	*Lunch*	*Dinner*
Day 1	**Fruity Swiss Muesli,** Yoghurt Fruit	**Annabel's Tasty Beefburgers** with vegetables **Pear, Apple and Raspberry Crumble** with custard	**Two Tomato Pasta Sauce Frozen Strawberry Yoghurt Ice-Cream**
Day 2	Cheese on toast **Apricot, Apple and Pear Custard**	**Grandma's Tasty Fish Pie** Fruit	**Chicken Fillets with Mango Chutney and Apricots** with vegetables **Poached Fruits**
Day 3	Porridge with honey or jam Apple purée *Petit Suisse*	**Marinated Chicken on the Griddle** with vegetables and chips **Annabel's Bread and Butter Pudding**	**Bow-Ties with Gruyère and Cherry Tomatoes** Fruit and ice-cream
Day 4	Scrambled eggs Cereal Fruit	**Chicken and Apple Balls Snow-Covered Fruit Salad**	**Nursery Fish Pie Cranberry and Raspberry Jelly**
Day 5	**Pineapple and Raisin Muffins** Yoghurt Fruit	**Shepherd's Pie** with vegetables **Strawberry Rice Pudding**	**Mini Pizzas with Puff Pastry Base** Fruit
Day 6	Boiled eggs with fingers of toast Prunes Yoghurt	**Cod in a Cheese Sauce with Matchstick Vegetables Cranberry and Raspberry Jelly**	**Bow-Ties with Tomato and Mozzarella Sauce** Fruit and ice-cream
Day 7	Cereal Cheese Fruit	**Marinated Chicken on the Griddle** with vegetables and baked potato **Pear, Apple and Raspberry Crumble**	**Tuna Tagliatelle Peaches with Amaretto Biscuits**

These meal charts show you how to plan ahead and cook for the whole family together.

FAMILY MEAL PLANNER

	Breakfast	Lunch	Dinner
Day 1	**Fruity Swiss Muesli** Yoghurt	**Bow-Ties with Tomato and Mozzarella Sauce**	**Annabel's Tasty Beefburgers** with vegetables and potato **Pear, Apple and Raspberry Crumble** with custard
Day 2	Cheese on toast **Apricot, Apple and Pear Custard**	**Chicken and Apple Balls** with vegetables	**Grandma's Tasty Fish Pie** with vegetables **Snow-Covered Fruit Salad**
Day 3	**French Toast Cut-Outs** Baked beans	**Grandma's Gefilte Fish** or **Tasty Fish Pie** with salad Fruit	**Marinated Chicken on the Griddle** and baked potato with salad **Frozen Strawberry Yoghurt Ice Cream** or yoghurt and fruit
Day 4	Scrambled egg Cereal	**Vegetarian Rissoles** or **Chicken and Apple Balls** Fruit salad	**My Favourite Pasta with Broccoli** **Home-Made Fruit Jelly** and ice cream
Day 5	**Pineapple and Raisin Muffins** Yoghurt and honey	**Cod in a Cheese Sauce with Matchstick Vegetables**	**Shepherd's Pie** with vegetables or salad **Poached Fruits**
Day 6	**The Three Bears' Breakfast** Prunes	**Tuna Bake with Potato Crisps** Fruit	**Mini Minute Steaks** with potato **Home-Made Fruit Jelly** and ice cream
Day 7	**Cheese Scramble** and toast Fruit	**Stir-Fried Chicken** or **Bar-B-Q Chicken** with vegetables **Annabel's Bread and Butter Pudding**	**Gratin of Sole** **Ratatouille**

INDEX

ACKNOWLEDGEMENTS

I am indebted to the following people for their help and advice during the writing of this book.

Dr Stephen Herman FRCP, Consultant Paediatrician, Central Middlesex Hospital.
Margaret Lawson, Senior Lecturer in Paediatric Nutrition, Institute of Child Health.
Professor Charles Brook, Consultant Paediatric Endocrinologist, Middlesex Hospital.
Dr Sam Tucker FRCP, Consultant Paediatrician, Hillingdon Hospital.
Jacky Bernett, Community Dietician.
Dr Tim Lobstein, specialist in children's food and nutrition at The London Food Commission.
Carol Nock SRN FCN, Midwife.
Kathy Morgan, State Registered Health Visitor.
My mother, Evelyn Etkind, for all her encouragement in writing this book.
David Karmel, for his patience in teaching me how to use a computer.
Beryl Lewsey, for her enthusiasm and hard work.
Ros Edwards, Ian Jackson, Susan Fleming, Fiona Eves and Elaine Partington of Eddison Sadd.
Dr Irving Etkind, for his help in research.
Jane Hamilton, my nanny, for restraining my children from wiping out my manuscript on the computer!
And, most important of all, my husband Simon, my chief guinea pig, for all his support.

The Author

Annabel Karmel is a leading author on cooking for children. After the death of her first child, who died of a rare viral disease aged just under three months, Annabel wrote *The Complete Baby and Toddler Meal Planner*, which is now an international bestseller. Annabel has written eight other books on feeding children including *Superfoods For Babies and Children* and *Annabel Karmel's Family Meal Planner*.

Annabel lives in London and is the mother of three children, Nicholas, Lara and Scarlett. As a trained cordon bleu cook and young mother, she experienced first-hand the difficulties in feeding young children. She thoroughly researched all aspects of feeding babies and children to cut through the often confusing and conflicting advice given to parents on the subject. She combined her findings with her own experience and knowledge of cooking, testing each recipe on a panel of babies and toddlers.

Annabel writes regularly for magazines and newspapers, including *The Times* and *The Daily Express* and appears frequently on television.

EDDISON•SADD EDITIONS

Editors Sophie Bevan, Fiona Eves and Susan Fleming
Proofreader Nikky Twyman
Indexer Heather Thomas
Art Director Elaine Partington
Mac Designer Brazzle Atkins
Production Karyn Claridge and Charles James